COOK 1.0

COOK 1.0

a fresh approach to the **vegetarian** kitchen

BREAKFAST, LUNCH + DINNER

HEIDI SWANSON

foreword by **Art Smith**, best-selling author of *Back to the Table*

STEWART, TABORI & CHANG · NEW YORK

Published in 2004 by
Stewart, Tabori & Chang
115 West 18th Street
New York, NY 10011

Canadian Distribution:
Canadian Manda Group
One Atlantic Avenue,
Suite 105, Toronto, Ontario
M6K 3E7 Canada

Library of Congress
Cataloging-in-
Publication Data

Swanson, Heidi, 1973-
Cook 1.0 : a fresh approach
to the vegetarian kitchen /
Heidi Swanson ; foreword
by Art Smith.
p. cm.
Includes index.
ISBN 1-58479-335-X
(hardcover)
1. Vegetarian cookery.
I. Title: Fresh approach to
the vegetarian kitchen.
II. Title.
TX837.S96 2004
641.5'636—dc22
2004007831

Design: Paul G. Wagner
Editorial: Jennifer Lang
Production: Kim Tyner

Printed in China

10 9 8 7 6 5 4 3 2 1
First Printing

Stewart, Tabori & Chang is
a subsidiary of

LA MARTINIÈRE
GROUPE

Acknowledgments

Thanks to my family for accepting the monstrous green and purple cake creations of a seven-year-old with nothing but smiles, love, and encouragement. I'd also like to thank each of the following individuals for their encouragement, enthusiasm, inspiration, feedback, and many contributions. I've loved every moment of working on this book and look forward to enjoying many meals with each of you in the future.

Chris Anderson, Wayne Bremser, Michael Broussard, Ryan Courier, Shay Curley, Hadley and Philip Fierlinger, Ross Fubini, Audra Johnson, Heather Gibbs, Lanha Hong-Porretta, Jennifer Lang, Jen Luan, Katherine and Janet McCartney, Jason Michaels, Kathleen Miller, Whitney Moss, Quyen Nguyen, Art Smith, Tiffany Spencer, Jennifer Streit, Kim Tyner, and Paul Wagner.

contents

FOREWORD : 9

INTRODUCTION : 10
about this book / stockpile / equipment / basics

CHAPTER 1.0
BREAKFAST : 18
smoothies / fruit bowls / drop biscuits / pancakes / frittatas

CHAPTER 2.0
LUNCHBOX : 38
panini / quesadillas / pocket tarts / savory kabobs / thin-crust pizzas

CHAPTER 3.0
ONE-DISH DINNERS : 62
pot pies / rice bowls / fondues / stir-fries / pasta dishes / risottos

CHAPTER 4.0
SIDES : 88
green salads / smooth soups / chunky chowders / mashed potatoes / roasted vegetables

CHAPTER 5.0
SPREADS, SAUCES + SALSAS : 112
dips / flavored butters / sauces / salsas / vinaigrettes

CHAPTER 6.0
SWEETS : 134
shortcakes / tarts / sherbets / vanilla gelato with toppings / tuiles / cobblers

CHAPTER 7.0
DRINKS : 160
spritzers / iced teas / lemonades / sangrías / margaritas

CHAPTER 8.0
IDEAS : 178
garnishes / tabletop / menus / flavor combinations

RESOURCES : 186
CONVERSION CHARTS : 187
INDEX : 188

foreword

Every modern family faces challenges and dilemmas every day. Given the hectic pace we all keep, we seek safety and comfort at the end of the day. We're looking for refuge from the hustle and bustle of the outside world.

The one place we know can be counted on to provide this much-needed safe haven is our home. It is there that we can be ourselves and shut out the stresses of everyday life. But often, even as we settle into our comfort zone, we are faced with the age-old question: What will we eat for dinner? Ideally, we want a meal that tastes great, isn't complicated, and keeps us healthy. I get letters from the four corners of the world seeking advice on how to feed a family well, and this tells me that families everywhere need a little practical guidance on the subject.

Being a personal chef has given me the opportunity to really understand families' needs firsthand. My job is to simplify life for the busy family by taking the guesswork and complexity out of the kitchen. I don't believe in complicated food that keeps us from the table. Nourishment should be both delicious and good for us and not too hard to make. I am constantly on the lookout for ways to make my own life, as well as those of my adopted families, easier. I, like Heidi Swanson, have several hundred cookbooks that I rarely use. I don't have a degree from a culinary school. I do have, however, a career that allows me to really understand what makes families happy.

Anyone with a kitchen and hungry friends and family needs this book. Heidi takes away so much of the anxiety cooking can create and offers an organized, sensible solution by making her recipes easier to follow. Her charts make these recipes uniquely user friendly: Instead of reading through paragraphs of instructions, one quick glance will tell you what you'll need to do. Once you become familiar with her style, you will understand that she "holds the keys to the cooking kingdom."

For too many years to count, medical professionals have been telling their patients that a healthful vegetarian diet can prevent problems that can lead to serious illness. We need books like this one because it destroys the stereotype of vegetarian food as dull, bland, and uninspired. When vegetarian diets first entered the mainstream in the '60s and '70s, the highlights were hummus, sprouts, and mushy veggie burgers. Heidi has brought this cuisine into the next century, giving us a whole new look at meat-free living. Who wouldn't love to taste dishes like Red-Leaf Salad with Pomegranate Vinaigrette; Brie, Apple-Cranberry + Fake Bacon Panini, or Wild Rice Bowl with Dried Cranberries? And Heidi doesn't skimp on sweets. She includes several takes on shortcake, including my personal favorite, Classic Strawberry Shortcake.

Cook 1.0 is not just a cookbook; it's a twenty-first-century tool that takes America's families and those living elsewhere on a culinary journey. This book will teach families how and what to eat and help them live fuller, more balanced lives, and its wide variety of inventive recipes will take the mystery out of vegetarian cooking. Thank you, Heidi, for creating a book that makes eating sensibly easier than it's ever been.

Let us celebrate this superb vegetarian cookbook. Mothers have been telling their children for centuries to eat their vegetables. Heidi has honored that age-old request by making it a whole lot easier to do just that. So America, eat your vegetables; Heidi has made them taste better than ever!

– Art Smith

* * *

INTRODUCTION

about this book / stockpile /
equipment / basics

about this book

I'm not entirely sure that I have any business writing a cookbook. I've never attended culinary school, and I don't run a fancy restaurant. I still cry an embarrassing amount when I cut onions, I'm a wimp when it comes to touching hot surfaces (no asbestos fingers here), and plead guilty to the charge of not being able to rattle off the names of every apple varietal in the United States. I have a cheap but well-liked five-piece knife set from IKEA and a hand-me-down Cuisinart food processor from my dad circa the 1980s, both of which have seen their day.

My guess is that I am like many of you when it comes to cooking. I may cook more often, but the way I approach the kitchen is decidedly ordinary. I cook my favorite recipes over and over. I have a mental list of my favorite ingredients, and I have a palette of cooking techniques that I'm comfortable with. One thing about me that isn't so ordinary is that I own many, many cookbooks, vintage and contemporary. Oddly enough, very few seemed to speak to the way I wanted to approach the kitchen. I decided to develop a fresh approach to the way a cookbook could be written and organized.

This is not your ordinary cookbook

Cook 1.0 reflects a new way of thinking about recipes and approaching cooking for the beginning contemporary home cook. It's also a unique way of using cookbooks. This book includes basic recipes and methods for breakfast, lunch, and dinner dishes, sides, sauces, desserts, and drinks, and then provides easy-to-read tables to show delicious and inventive ways to build on those recipes. This mix-and-match culinary strategy allows you to personalize recipes based on local ingredients, family preference, and available preparation time.

The majority of cookbooks today showcase a given chef's (or culinary professional's) view of what food should be. For the new cook, cookbooks can often be overwhelming, loaded with complex recipes, extensive ingredient lists, long preparation times, and obscure, hard-to-find items.

Cook 1.0 is written for cooks who generally want to spend less than an hour in the kitchen each night, but also want to eat like they spent four. You'll learn how to get the most out of your time in the kitchen by using the freezer, creating large batches, and utilizing ingredients you have on hand in creative ways. Don't be put off by the lack of standard ingredient lists in this book; when you're ready to pull together a shopping list, just scan across a recipe and all your ingredients will look like **this**.

A gradual vegetarian

I didn't become vegetarian overnight, but I do wish I had become vegetarian earlier. As a teenager I was under the assumption that being vegetarian meant two things: not eating meat, and a diet consisting primarily of vegetable greens (which I now love). Over the years, as meat began to make up less and less of my overall diet, my eyes began to open to an entire world of amazing grains, greens, pastas, fruits, beans, cheeses, and spices.

A broad range of people, young and old, have embraced a vegetarian diet for individual reasons, from moral issues to taste preference to health. Personally, as a vegetarian I feel healthier and more confident about what I'm eating on a daily basis. For me, being vegetarian is just part of an overall awareness of where my food comes from and how its production affects the world around me.

As you will see, being vegetarian doesn't mean a strict diet of hummus, brown rice, and lentils served on a tie-dyed placemat. This book is packed with contemporary flavors and uses tasty ingredients that will appeal to vegetarians and nonvegetarians alike. A few of my favorite recipes, the ones I can't do without, include Citrus Risotto (page 86), Red Pepper + Lemon Kabobs (page 54), and Brie, Apple-Cranberry + Fake Bacon Panini (page 42). And nothing beats starting off the day with a stack of Banana-Macadamia Pancakes (page 32).

The recipes

I'm pretty loose when it comes to cooking. I love to throw in a pinch of this and a splash of that, and I encourage you to do the same as you gain confidence in your cooking. Trust your instincts as well as your taste buds. I'm not going to tell you that your instincts will always be right (mine aren't always on the money), but the more new recipes you try, the sooner your instincts and abilities will blossom. Many of the charts in this book started out as a favorite basic recipe – I would tweak and adapt it to my liking with different ingredients and flavors, and then make notes on my favorite variations.

The kind of food I cook every day is good, fresh, simple, and quick to pull together. There are lazy days when I love to spend all afternoon cooking. It's fun to make homemade marshmallows or fresh buns for a BBQ, but when I'm busy that doesn't always fly. Regardless of time constraints and day-to-day commitments, I find it invigorating to take the time to cook and enjoy delicious food with my friends and family, even if some meals need to be quicker than others. The recipes in this book have been collected with this in mind, and most of them can be prepared with minimal fuss.

Keep in mind that feeling stressed out and under pressure in the kitchen is no fun. It's important to keep a positive perspective on your kitchen creations. I try to keep cooking an enjoyable and creative outlet for myself, always learning and sharing with everyone around me. More important, I try to keep it casual. That's not to say I don't do special things, but when I have friends over, I don't fuss over fancy individual platings and polished silver. I like to put friends to work chopping and rinsing, serve plates up family-style with simple tableware, and focus my attention on the people and tasty food around me. One of the things I do to add a bit of a twist is to make at least one dish using an ingredient that my friends may not have tried before, such as hibiscus, fresh garbanzo beans, mulled wine, or citron. I also try to revive certain culinary trends (such as fondue) that may have fallen out of fashion and then add a contemporary twist. This keeps me on my toes and always learning about new techniques, ingredients, and flavors.

Inspiration

My family played a huge role in my eventual culinary curiosity with their encouragement and enthusiasm. I grew up in a food-loving family where holiday seasons meant exchanging gifts that consisted almost exclusively of cookbooks, pots, baking pans, and an endless array of kitchen gadgets.

I still find inspiration close to home in San Francisco, where I live, within walking (and smelling) distance of scores of ethnic-food purveyors – Ethiopian, Thai, Japanese, Italian, Indian, Cuban, Mexican, Spanish, and Vietnamese. And when I travel, whether it's to a foreign country or just the next town over, I try to stop into the local library to look for new ideas, recipes, and techniques.

You will see many of these influences in the following chapters. I hope you enjoy making these dishes as much as I have.

Lessons my dad taught me about cooking

- Always start with a big sink full of hot soapy water.
- Invest in a couple of good-quality, thick-bottom pans.
- Set up your mise en place: Prep all your ingredients before you start cooking.
- Always use a sharp knife.
- Start with a clean kitchen and clean as you go along.
- If you get into good habits early, you will enjoy cooking more and more as you grow older.

stockpile

These are my tried and true staples. You will see them used over and over in my recipes. I keep all of the following on hand, and then shop for fresh ingredients as I need them.

Cheese

Many markets have vastly improved cheese selections now. Try to steer clear of the walls of bricked, plastic-sealed cheese hanging next to the yogurt in every supermarket in America. You can do better than that, and you don't have to spend much more money. I always use the best cheese I can find (or afford) at the time. If you only make two improvements to your cheese repertoire, shave your Parmesan yourself (it only takes a second with a Microplane grater) and buy fresh (buffalo) mozzarella.

Coconut milk

The faux dairy of the tropics, canned coconut milk is great because it isn't perishable. I keep a few cans of the "light" variety on hand for quick curries and soups.

Crushed tomatoes

I love canned crushed tomatoes and use them in everything from pasta sauce and pizza toppings to pot pie fillings and pocket tarts.

Dried fruits

The jewels of the pantry. Try to keep a variety of dried or special fruits on hand. Dried cranberries, apricots, pineapple, and crystallized ginger are all flavor-packed and colorful additions to many recipes.

Eggs

I like my eggs large, free-range, and as fresh as possible. Be sure to peek inside the carton before getting to the counter; I find cracked eggs all the time.

Extra-virgin olive oil

I keep bottles and bottles of extra-virgin olive oil on hand. I use it in absolutely everything, from salads and pastas to roasted vegetables and marinades. If a recipe calls for good-quality olive oil, it doesn't mean you have to buy the priciest one on the shelf. Sample a few over time and find the one you like best in a price range you're comfortable with. My favorite everyday extra-virgin olive oil costs about seven dollars for a big bottle.

Garlic, shallots, and onions

I always keep some of each on hand.

Nuts

I keep an entire drawer full of nuts in the refrigerator. My favorites are pine nuts, cashews, peanuts, walnuts, macadamias, and hazelnuts.

Olives

It's fairly commonplace to come across great olive bars in local supermarkets and specialty food shops. I always have a selection ready to throw into salads and pastas, or for a quick and easy guest snack. Don't get stuck in a rut; sample all different kinds of olives. Some of my favorites include kalamata, niçoise, and the big, meaty, oversized green ones.

Pasta

I keep all sorts of shapes and sizes of dried pasta noodles on hand – Asian noodles like udon and soba, too.

Pastes and sauces

Pastes and sauces are an easy way to add quick, delicious flavors to your recipes. I always have Thai curry pastes in red, green, and yellow. Hoisin and dark and light soy sauces are also great. Stock up at Asian markets, where you can find a selection of sauces on the cheap. I also like the little cans of chipotle peppers in adobo sauce for easy and convenient spicy, smoky heat.

Peanut oil

I keep a small bottle of peanut oil for stir-fries.

Rice

Jasmine, Arborio, and wild rices are a good place to start.

Salt

While there are many salts available today, I have a hands-down favorite for taste, price, and general availability: La Baleine sea salt. It comes in coarse- and fine-ground. I've tried both and for most uses I prefer the fine-ground variety; it absorbs more quickly into the food and you don't end up crunching on big grains of salt.

Spices

I try to grind or grate my own spices. The spices you buy in a jar from the store can be, at best, flat tasting, and at worst, musky or stale. I try to keep nutmeg, cinnamon, cayenne, red-pepper flakes, saffron threads, and whole vanilla beans on hand.

Unsalted butter

Load up on good quality organic butter when you see it go on sale, often around the holidays. I keep boxes in the freezer and thaw sticks out when needed.

equipment

I don't believe for a minute that you need to have ultra-fancy kitchen gear and gadgets to be an exceptional cook, but the following is a list of kitchen equipment I would have a tough time doing without.

Baking sheets
I have two or three of these. I use them to bake cookies, roast vegetables, prep pizzas, and as a spill guard when I'm making things that have a tendency to boil over in the oven, like pot pies or cobblers. I've learned the hard way that it's easier to clean a baking sheet than an oven.

Blender
If you're serious about slushy drinks or morning smoothies, there is no getting around having a blender. I also use mine for making dips, tapenades, soups, sauces, and a delicious, bright green Pesto Sauce (page 126).

Colander
Don't even try to function in the kitchen without one. You'll need it to drain pasta and rinse vegetables and salad greens.

Cookie cutters
A great way to add a bit of whimsy and charm to your cooking. I especially love the tiny ones. I have a butterfly set that I use all the time to put an unexpected touch on tarts, pies, and cookies.

Cutting board
Your counter and knives will thank you.

Electric mixer and food processor
Many recipes are now written with the assumption that most kitchens have one or both of these. Luxury items for some people, necessities for others. I fall somewhere in between. I certainly give my

KitchenAid mixer a regular workout and use it for all sorts of cookie, pizza, and bread doughs. In general, though, I like to chop, so I have to think hard about whether or not I'll want to clean an appliance before I go ahead and use it.

Knives
If you have cheap knives, at least make sure they aren't dull. Try to find knives that are well suited to the size and shape of your hands. I use one of the following two knives ninety percent of the time:
Serrated knife. This is the one with teeth. I use this knife to cut bread, tomatoes, and sometimes lettuce.
Big chopping knife. I use this knife for almost everything else: chopping and mincing everything from garlic and onions to vegetables or tofu.

Measuring spoons and cups
As much as I like to cook with a pinch of this and a dash of that, I rely heavily on measuring spoons when embarking on any dish for which the exact amount really matters, like making pizza dough.

Microplane grater
This has saved me countless hours and endless grated knuckles. If you invest in only one kitchen gadget, let this be it. I use it for everything from grating Parmesan to zesting limes to making chocolate shavings. It's one of the few things in my kitchen I use absolutely every day.

Oven thermometer
I will admit I didn't buy one of these until I started getting serious about writing this book. It was ten dollars, and I should have shelled out the cash for it much earlier. It allows you to see if your oven is running hot or cold. Luckily, my oven and I have

an amicable give-and-take relationship: It pumps out accurate temperatures as long as I keep her well cleaned and shiny.

Parchment paper or silicone baking mat
Truth be told, I still use parchment more often than the fancy silicone mats. Using either is easier than cleaning a baking sheet, and both provide perfect nonstick protection for your baking endeavors.

Pots
Now this is serious. You need a couple good pans that are thick on the bottom so you don't scorch food. I have a mishmash of nonstick and regular (so I don't need to worry about scraping off the nonstick coating). I use my big saucepan, a big sauté pan, and a couple of smaller ones the majority of the time. I think you can do quite well with just four pots.

Tart and cake pans and muffin tins
I have a few of each of these in a various sizes and shapes. If you're anything like me, you probably never have the exact size a recipe calls for. I usually just fill whatever pan or tin I have that's closest or smaller in size, save any leftover batter or dough (or make a tiny tart or cake on the side), keep a close eye on it in the oven, and hope for the best.

Wooden spoon
A kitchen icon for good reason. It's great for stirring and easy on your nonstick cookware.

basics

These are the little quickie recipes I use for everyday eats and add-ins.

Homemade Croutons

Making your own croutons adds an extra-special touch to a salad. The alternative, store-bought croutons, are mostly mediocre.

The following recipe for croutons is a super way to use up day-old bread. Leftovers can be sealed in an airtight plastic bag and used on salads throughout the week.

1/4 c. **extra-virgin olive oil**
3 cloves **garlic**, minced
A couple pinches of both **s+p**
About 6 cups quality day-old **bread** or baguette

Preheat the oven to 400°F. In a large mixing bowl, combine the oil, garlic, and s+p. Cut the bread into cubes or rounds, or just rip off small chunks. Put the bread pieces into the bowl with the oil and toss around for a minute, until the bread has a light coating of oil. Place the bread in a single layer on a baking sheet. Bake on the middle rack of the oven, flipping the croutons once or twice to make sure all sides are cooked, until the croutons are golden and crisp, about 10 minutes. Let cool, then season again with s+p to taste.

Roasted Garlic

Nothing could be easier than making roasted garlic. I usually make three or four heads at once so I have some on hand to squeeze onto a slice of baguette, stir into mashed potatoes, or spread on a pizza or sandwich. You can never have too much roasted garlic around.

3 or 4 heads **garlic** (all similar in size)
1 T. **extra-virgin olive oil**
A pinch of **salt**

Preheat the oven to 375°F. Tear off any loose skins and cut off the top third of the garlic heads, so you lob off just the very tops of the cloves.

Place the heads cut side up in a small baking dish, or on a large piece of aluminum foil. Drizzle the garlic with the oil and sprinkle it with salt. Cover or wrap it tightly in the foil and place the garlic in the oven on the middle rack. Cook for about 45 minutes, or until the cloves start to soften up and brown a bit. Uncover, and return the garlic to the oven until the cloves get mushy and there's a nice brown color on the outsides, 10 to 20 more minutes.

Sweetened Fresh Whipped Cream

Whipping heavy cream by hand is an arm workout for anyone, so I typically fire up my electric mixer when I hear a call for fresh whipped cream (which is often). I pour as much **heavy cream** into the mixing bowl as I think I'll need, usually a cup or two, and then sweeten it with **sugar** by the tablespoonful to taste. Typically, I use about 1 1/2 tablespoons of sugar per 1 cup cream. Start whipping!

I like my whipped cream floppy and just barely billowy. If you overwhip your cream, you'll know it — it starts to separate and go the way of butter.

Toasted Coconut Flakes

Preheat the oven to 350°F. Spread **coconut flakes** out on a baking sheet in an even layer. Place in the oven for 5 to 6 minutes, tossing every couple of minutes, until the coconut is golden brown.

If you're dealing with only a small quantity of coconut flakes, just place a thin layer in a skillet over medium heat. Toss regularly until the coconut is golden, about 5 minutes or so.

Toasted Nuts

You can toast nuts in the oven, or in a pan or skillet over medium-low heat. For most nuts, I opt for the skillet because it's quicker and easier to keep an eye on. The skillet works particularly well for toasting **pine nuts**, **walnuts**, and slivered **almonds**. Just shake them around every few minutes to get all sides nice and toasted.

The one nut I usually toast in the oven is the **hazelnut**. Preheat the oven to 350°F and place the hazelnuts, skins and all, on a rimmed baking sheet. Roast until the skins start to darken and the nuts become fragrant, about 10 minutes. Let them cool a bit. To remove the skins, place the toasted nuts in a clean cotton dish towel. Vigorously rub them around, and the skins will come right off.

CHAPTER 1.0

BREAKFAST

smoothies / fruit bowls / drop biscuits /
pancakes / frittatas

smoothies

Smoothies are a colorful and tasty way to kick off the day. They're also great on the go. Keep in mind, though, that not all smoothies are created equal: Too thick, too thin, and too warm are all common problems you run into when smoothies are a part of your ritual.

I'm picky when it comes to making great smoothies and have all sorts of opinions about what a top smoothie should be. Smoothies need to be ice cold and frosty – hold the room temperature fruit, please. They need to be thick and creamy, as opposed to watery and icy, with a minimum of seeds. I don't mind a few seeds, but there's a reason these drinks are called smoothies and not "crunchies."

The following recipes make extra-thick, frosty, flavorful smoothies that can be made in less than 5 minutes. The worst and most time-consuming part of making them, of course, is cleaning out the blender afterward.

tips

- *Keep in mind that your smoothie is only going to be as good as the fruit you put in it. I love to use the freshest, ripest organically grown produce I can find.*
- *I always freeze the fruit first so the resulting smoothie will have a nice, frozen slushy texture: Run berries and other fruits under a gentle stream of cold water to rinse any dirt off before freezing. Pat them dry with a paper towel to get rid of any extra water and then place them in the freezer.*

- *It's a shame to let any fruit in your house go bad and end up in the trash. If you see a banana or melon that's starting to get overripe, just slice it or cut it into 1-inch chunks and pop it into a freezer bag. This way you'll have a stockpile of frozen fruit, primed and ready for smoothie making.*
- *Let frozen fruit sit out on the counter for 5 minutes or so before making smoothies. It softens the fruit up just a bit so the blender doesn't have such a hard time doing its job.*
- *Smoothie popsicles make a great summertime treat. Pour a just-blended smoothie into popsicle molds and freeze them until they're solid.*

- *If you have a temperamental blender, add any liquid ingredients first, then softer ingredients, then the frozen ingredients. You may need to stop the blender, stir the ingredients, and push some of the chunks down toward the blade. Don't stick a spoon down into the middle of the blender while it's running.*
- *If you only have room-temperature fruit and don't have time to freeze it, go ahead and add ice cubes to the blender, one at a time, until you get the consistency and temperature you want.*

TYPE OF SMOOTHIE	COMBINE ALL INGREDIENTS IN A BLENDER
apple-a-day smoothie	▸ 2 c. **applesauce**, chilled ▸ 1 **banana**, sliced and frozen (about 1 c.) ▸ 1 c. **vanilla frozen yogurt** ▸ ¾ t. **cinnamon** Puree until smooth, 1 to 2 minutes.
honey bee smoothie	▸ 2 **peaches** or **nectarines**, sliced and frozen (about 2 c.) ▸ 1 **banana**, sliced and frozen (about 1 c.) ▸ 3 T. **honey** Puree until smooth, 1 to 2 minutes.
sunrise smoothie	▸ 1 **orange**, split into segments and frozen (about 1 c.) ▸ 1 **cantaloupe**, cubed and frozen (about 1 c.) ▸ 1 **banana**, sliced and frozen (about 1 c.) ▸ ½ c. **orange juice** ▸ ½ c. silken **tofu** (optional) ▸ 1 ½ T. **honey** Puree until smooth, 1 to 2 minutes.
triple-berry smoothie	▸ ⅔ c. **blackberries**, frozen ▸ ⅔ c. **strawberries**, frozen ▸ ⅔ c. **raspberries**, frozen ▸ 1 **banana**, sliced and frozen (about 1 c.) ▸ ½ c. **orange juice** Puree until smooth, 1 to 2 minutes. If your fruit is very seedy, you might want to push the mixture through a sieve.
tropical smoothie	▸ 1 medium **pineapple**, cubed and frozen (about 3 c.) ▸ 1 **banana**, sliced and frozen (about 1 c.) ▸ ½ c. **coconut nectar** (often found in the juice aisle). Puree until smooth, 1 to 2 minutes.
watermelon-lime smoothie	▸ ¼ or ⅓ **watermelon**, deseeded, cubed, and frozen (about 1 ½ c.) ▸ 1 ½ c. **strawberries**, frozen ▸ 1 c. **lime sorbet** ▸ 1 T. **honey** Puree until smooth, 1 to 2 minutes.

fruit bowls

For the early part of my life I was lukewarm about fruit salads, and with good reason. The fruit salad I typically encountered either came in a small tin can alongside my "hot lunch" in the school cafeteria or was of the creamy variety reserved for BBQs or potlucks, slathered in some sort of processed whipped topping.

Fortunately there are places like my favorite tiny pizzeria here in San Francisco, Pizzetta 211. It's on a quiet block of 23rd Avenue off Geary Boulevard, and everything there is handmade and has a rustic quality to it. Occasionally, if my timing is right, they will have a giant bowl of the most perfect berries sitting on the counter. You can smell them five feet away as you walk in, and they're served simply with a big dollop of slightly sweetened crème fraîche. Nothing could be better, a perfect example of the best kind food: simple, fresh, and unfussy.

The following recipes make beautiful bowls of jewel-like seasonal fruit inspired by some of the best fruit bowls I've tasted in the past, like the one at Pizzetta 211. I keep all the fruit bowl recipes simple, and only use a small assortment of perfect ingredients.

SELECTING THE PERFECT FRUIT You have to enlist all your senses to figure out whether or not a fruit is prime for eating. You're going to want to look at it, touch it, smell it, even listen to it. If you're lucky, many growers present at the farmers' markets might also encourage you to taste their wonderful samples.

Look at it: Many fruits look green if they're underripe. They look bruised, brown, and sometimes even have moldy spots as they go from ripe to overly ripe.

Touch it: Fruit that is hard to the touch and isn't supposed to be (such as mango, banana, or avocado) is probably underripe. The perfect fruit gives a bit of resistance. If it's mushy, or has soft spots, it's most likely overripe.

Smell it: This is particularly useful for fruits like melons and peaches. Put your nose to the stem end and smell. You want your fruit to have a nice, fragrant essence.

Listen to it: Lots of people believe that if you knock on a watermelon and hear a hollow sound it's a good indication of a tasty, ripe melon.

Taste it: We've all had unripe fruit. It's often tough to chew, bitter, and flavorless – pretty much inedible. Overly ripe fruit can be mushy in the mouth and sometimes has a fermented taste.

If you still aren't sure if the fruit is good, don't be afraid to ask questions. The grocers at the market are usually happy to offer guidance.

tips

- *Get your hands on as much of the freshest organic, locally grown produce as you can.*

- *Don't be afraid to ask the markets or stores you shop at what day of the week they get their shipments in. This way you're most likely to get the very best, freshest ingredients possible.*

- *If you're at the store and the type of produce you're after looks less than appealing, ask someone who works there. They sometimes have fresher fruit and produce in the back.*

STEP	1	2	3
TYPE OF FRUIT BOWL	MAKE MARINADE OR TOPPING	COMBINE FRUITS	ADD FINISHING TOUCHES
berry fruit bowl	Whip up a batch of **Sweetened Fresh Whipped Cream** (page 16).	In a medium bowl, gently combine perfectly ripe, gently rinsed and dried berries: ▸ 1 c. **blackberries** ▸ 1 c. **raspberries** ▸ 1 c. **blueberries**	Serve mixed berries in individual bowls with a dollop of the whipped cream.
citrus fruit bowl	Squeeze the juice of 1 **orange** and set aside.	In a medium bowl, gently combine 3 to 4 c. mixed citrus segments. Try to use a mix of colors and tastes (sweet and tart). I like to combine: ▸ 1 **pomelo** ▸ 1 **red grapefruit** ▸ 1 **tangerine** ▸ 2 **navel oranges** To easily cut citrus into wedges, start by cutting off the two ends of the fruit. Carve off the skin and the pith all the way around. Now that all you have is the fruit, carefully slice right next to the membrane of each segment so the wedges come out intact.	Toss with the orange juice and serve. Great with breakfast or as a snack on hot days.
melon bowl	Squeeze the juice of: ▸ ½ **lemon** ▸ ½ **lime** Set aside.	In a medium bowl, gently combine: ▸ 1 ½ c. cubed seeded **cantaloupe** or any orange-fleshed melon (1-inch cubes) ▸ 1 ½ c. **honeydew melon** or any green-fleshed melon (1-inch cubes) ▸ 1 c. peeled and thinly sliced **jícama**	Toss the melons and jicama with the lemon and lime juice. Add a pinch of **salt** and a pinch of **cayenne pepper**, and gently toss again before serving.
summer fruit bowl	Whip up a batch of **Sweetened Fresh Whipped Cream** (page 16). Toast ½ c. slivered **almonds** (see page 16).	In a medium bowl, gently combine: ▸ 2 c. stemmed and pitted sweet **cherries** ▸ 1 to 2 **apricots** and/or peaches, pitted and sliced into sixths or eighths (1 to 2 c.)	Toss the fruit with the toasted almonds. Serve with a dollop of the whipped cream. You can also skip the cream and serve fruit as a healthy side with a bowl of oatmeal or granola in the morning.

BERRY FRUIT BOWL

BASIC DROP BISCUITS

drop biscuits MAKES 18 BIG BISCUITS OR 36 MINIS

There is an ongoing debate in my family about biscuits. Since I'm from a family where most things are made from scratch, I find it interesting that when I go home, biscuits are now mostly made from a mix. Growing up we had tall, beautiful, golden homemade biscuits cut into perfect circles a few times a week. Biscuits with eggs for breakfast, leftovers for lunch. A big tray of them would sit there on the kitchen counter all day until there was nothing left but a crumb or two.

I can't remember exactly when it changed, but it was around the same time the warehouse superstores opened in our area; all of a sudden we had giant boxes of biscuit mix and vacuum-sealed ready-made biscuit cylinders.

The biscuits didn't taste as good. They didn't smell as good. They were sometimes a little too shiny and didn't smell like a simple mix of flour, butter, salt, and milk coming out of the oven.

So, the debate: To use mix or not to use mix? For a while, my father thought that biscuits made from a mix came out just as nicely as biscuits made from scratch. Here's my take: You can throw together an excellent homemade biscuit dough in less than five minutes, with five

ingredients. So why not go for it? Make extra and freeze some. By starting from scratch you're able to choose ingredients at a base level — you can use all organic flours, organic butter, and local dairy. You can choose milk from cows that haven't been injected with hormones and antibiotics, and you can use flour that hasn't been showered with pesticides. The better your ingredients, the better your biscuits.

I'm going to tell you right now that these biscuits aren't easy on the waistline. There are plenty of low-fat recipes in this book. These biscuits aren't among them. I figure if you're going to eat biscuits, just go for it. I did try to cut the butter back to ¾ cup, and the resulting biscuits weren't nearly as light or flaky.

These biscuits are quick and difficult to mess up. They're drop biscuits, so you don't have to roll them out. Just drop them onto a baking sheet the way you would with cookie dough. You'll end up with a nice flaky biscuit, with a slight crunchy golden crust and bottom. They're also used as the base recipe for the Shortcakes (pages 136-138) and Cobblers (pages 156-159) later on in this book.

tips

- Whatever you do, don't overmix your dough. You'll beat all the tender flakiness out of your biscuits.
- Cookie-cutter biscuits are a lot of fun. Cut back on the milk a bit and you can roll these biscuits out and cut them into circles, stars, hearts — just about any shape. Knead the dough just a few times, roll it ½-inch thick on a floured surface, and start cutting.

- If you have any leftover uncooked dough, just label it and save it in the freezer. Thaw it overnight in the refrigerator and you're only a few minutes away from a fresh batch of homemade biscuits first thing in the morning.
- Leftover cooked biscuits are easily reheated in the oven or toaster oven, but I prefer baking them to order.
- These make great lids for pot pies and savory cobblers. Just dollop a few tablespoons of

biscuit dough onto any soup, stew, or chili; make sure you're using an ovenproof bowl. Pop it into a preheated oven at 375°F for 20 minutes or so, until the biscuits are nice and golden brown.
- If you want a slight glaze on your biscuits, brush the tops lightly with egg whites before putting them in the oven.

STEP	1	2	3	4
TYPE OF BISCUIT	COMBINE DRY INGREDIENTS	CUT BUTTER INTO DRY INGREDIENTS	ADD MILK + EXTRAS	BAKE
basic drop biscuits	Preheat oven to 425°F. Into a large bowl or food processor, sift: ▸ 4 c. **unbleached all-purpose flour** ▸ 1½ t. **salt** ▸ 2 T. **baking powder**	To dry ingredients add: ▸ 1 c. chilled **unsalted butter**, cut into ¼-inch chunks Using a pastry cutter or 25 quick pulses of the food processor, blend until the mixture resembles tiny, sandy pebbles.	With a fork, stir in the following, until just combined: ▸ 2 c. **milk** (low-fat is fine)	Drop by heaping tablespoonfuls onto an ungreased nonstick baking sheet. Bake on the middle rack of the oven until the tops and bottoms are golden, roughly 12 minutes.
chive + goat cheese biscuits	Preheat oven to 425°F. Into a large bowl or food processor, sift: ▸ 4 c. **unbleached all-purpose flour** ▸ 1½ t. **salt** ▸ 2 T. **baking powder**	To dry ingredients add: ▸ 1 c. chilled **unsalted butter**, cut into ¼-inch chunks Using a pastry cutter or 25 quick pulses of the food processor, blend until the mixture resembles tiny, sandy pebbles.	With a fork, stir in the following, until just combined: ▸ 2 c. **milk** (low-fat is fine) ▸ ⅓ c. snipped **chives** ▸ ½ c. crumbled **goat cheese**	Drop by heaping tablespoonfuls onto an ungreased nonstick baking sheet. Bake on the middle rack of the oven until the tops and bottoms are golden, roughly 12 minutes.

cinnamon + spice biscuits	Preheat oven to 425°F. Into a large bowl or food processor, sift:
	▸ 4 c. **unbleached all-purpose flour**
	▸ 1½ t. **salt**
	▸ 2 T. **baking powder**
	▸ 1 t. **cinnamon**
	▸ ⅛ t. ground **cloves**
	▸ ¼ t. **nutmeg**, freshly ground
		To dry ingredients add:
		▸ 1 c. chilled **unsalted butter**, cut into ¼-inch chunks
		Using a pastry cutter or 25 quick pulses of the food processor, blend until the mixture resembles tiny, sandy pebbles.
			With a fork, stir in the following, until just combined:
			▸ 2 c. **milk** (low-fat is fine)
				Drop by heaping tablespoonfuls onto an ungreased nonstick baking sheet.
				  Bake on the middle rack of the oven until the tops and bottoms are golden, roughly 12 minutes.
				  Drizzle with **honey**.

citrus biscuits	Preheat oven to 425° F. Into a large bowl or food processor, sift: ▸ 4 c. **unbleached all-purpose flour** ▸ 1½ t. **salt** ▸ 2 T. **baking powder**	To dry ingredients add: ▸ 1 c. chilled **unsalted butter**, cut into ¼-inch chunks Using a pastry cutter or 25 quick pulses of the food processor, blend until the mixture resembles tiny, sandy pebbles.	With a fork, stir in the following, until just combined: ▸ 2 c. **milk** (low-fat is fine) ▸ Zest of 1 **lemon** ▸ Zest of 3 **oranges**	Drop by heaping tablespoonfuls onto an ungreased nonstick baking sheet. Bake on the middle rack of the oven until the tops and bottoms are golden, roughly 12 minutes.

STEP	1	2	3	4
TYPE OF BISCUIT	COMBINE DRY INGREDIENTS	CUT BUTTER INTO DRY INGREDIENTS	ADD MILK + EXTRAS	BAKE

cornmeal biscuits	*Preheat oven to 425°F. Into a large bowl or food processor, sift:*
	 ► *3 ½ c. **unbleached all-purpose flour***
	 ► *1 ½ t. **salt***
	 ► *2 T. **baking powder***
	 ► *½ c. finely-ground **cornmeal**.*
		To dry ingredients add:
		 ► *1 c. chilled **unsalted butter**, cut into ¼-inch chunks*
		 Using a pastry cutter or 25 quick pulses of the food processor, blend until the mixture resembles tiny, sandy pebbles.
			With a fork, stir in the following, until just combined:
			 ► *2 c. **milk** (low-fat is fine).*
				Drop by heaping tablespoonfuls onto an ungreased nonstick baking sheet.
				   *Brush the biscuit tops with a bit of **egg white** and sprinkle with a dusting of cornmeal.*
				   Bake on the middle rack of the oven until the tops and bottoms are golden, roughly 12 minutes.

honey biscuits	*Preheat oven to 425°F. Into a large bowl or food processor, sift:* ► *4 c. **unbleached all-purpose flour*** ► *1 ½ t. **salt*** ► *2 T. **baking powder***	*To dry ingredients add:* ► *1 c. chilled **unsalted butter**, cut into ¼-inch chunks* *Using a pastry cutter or 25 quick pulses of the food processor, blend until the mixture resembles tiny, sandy pebbles.*	*With a fork, stir in the following, until just combined:* ► *2 c. **milk** (low-fat is fine)* ► *½ c. **honey*** ► *½ c. **crystallized ginger** minced (optional)*	*Drop by heaping tablespoonfuls onto an ungreased nonstick baking sheet.* *Bake on the middle rack of the oven until the tops and bottoms are golden, roughly 12 minutes.*
parmesan + basil biscuits	*Preheat oven to 425°F. Into a large bowl or food processor, sift:* ► *4 c. **unbleached all-purpose flour*** ► *1 ½ t. **salt*** ► *2 T. **baking powder***	*To dry ingredients add:* ► *1 c. chilled **unsalted butter**, cut into ¼-inch chunks* *Using a pastry cutter or 25 quick pulses of the food processor, blend until the mixture resembles tiny, sandy pebbles.*	*With a fork, stir in the following, until just combined:* ► *2 c. **milk** (low-fat is fine)* ► *½ c. freshly grated **Parmesan cheese*** ► *½ c. slivered fresh **basil***	*Drop by heaping tablespoonfuls onto an ungreased nonstick baking sheet.* *Bake on the middle rack of the oven until the tops and bottoms are golden, roughly 12 minutes.*

pancakes MAKES ENOUGH TO FEED A SMALL CROWD, ABOUT 12 LARGE PANCAKES

A sunrise greeting of a big stack of hot pancakes is a great way to ease into the morning. Growing up in California, my parents would pile my sister and me into our wood-paneled Jeep Cherokee every summer and head off on the six-hour drive to Lake Tahoe. A solid two weeks of sunshine, pine trees, waterskiing, and crawdad fishing awaited us. Every morning my dad would either make a big stack of pancakes for us or drive down the road for fresh doughnuts, which we would eat out on the porch while we tossed crumbs to the chipmunks and squirrels.

I was shooting for a very simple pancake method here. Milk, flour, a single leavener, a bit of sugar, and an egg or two – the kind of pancake recipe where you could open your refrigerator on an average Saturday morning and have all the ingredients on hand for an amazing stack of pancakes. Since I rarely have buttermilk in my refrigerator (unless I've been baking), I was trying for a buttermilk-free recipe – no such luck. I tried just about every combination of those five ingredients possible and always ended up with gummy, dense, and sometimes deflated pancakes. I mean, some were good, but certainly not amazing.

So I swapped in the buttermilk and added a touch of baking soda. I ended up with a stunning pile of light, golden, puffy pancakes. This may be the only pancake recipe you'll ever need. As a bonus, I keep the batter nice and thick so I can easily control the shape of the pancakes on the grill.

tips

- *Resist the urge to overmix your batter. You will end up with tough pancakes.*
- *For easy pouring, put the batter in a small pitcher.*
- *Don't worry if the first pancake of a batch is messed up. This happens to everyone. Toss it out and get on with the next one.*
- *Keep an eye on your skillet temperature: You want to make sure it's hot enough, but not too hot. I usually have to play around with the temperature while I'm cooking.*

Too hot and your pancakes will scorch and have dark patches alongside very light patches.
- *If you've got kids in the house, have fun with shapes. You can pour your batter into a gallon-sized resealable plastic bag, cut off the tip of one corner, and pipe the batter into different shapes on the pan or skillet. There are also special pancake molds available in the shape of everything from hearts to clouds to autumn leaves.*

- *Keep your pancakes hot. While you're cooking the rest of the batch, toss the already-cooked pancakes into a baking dish and place in a warmish oven, 175°F or so. Leave the oven door open so the pancakes don't dry out.*
- *Serve the pancakes on warm plates with warm syrup.*
- *Freeze leftover pancakes and, when you want one for a snack, pop it in the toaster for a quick reheat. Not as good as fresh off the griddle, but still a tasty treat.*

STEP	1	2	3	4
TYPE OF PANCAKES	COMBINE DRY INGREDIENTS	ADD WET INGREDIENTS	COOK PANCAKES	FINISHING TOUCHES
basic buttermilk pancakes	In a large bowl, combine: ▸ 2 c. **unbleached all-purpose flour** ▸ 1 t. **baking powder** ▸ ½ t. **baking soda** ▸ ⅓ c. **sugar** ▸ A pinch of **salt**	To dry ingredients, add: ▸ 2 c. **buttermilk** ▸ 2 large **eggs**, lightly beaten ▸ 2 T. **unsalted butter**, melted Stir all the ingredients together until they are just combined. It's okay if the batter is a bit lumpy. Don't overmix.	Heat your skillet or pan to medium-hot and brush it with a bit of butter. If a drop of water dropped onto the pan starts to dance, you are in the ballpark. Slowly pour about ⅓ c. of the batter onto the skillet. Wait until the pancake bottom is deep golden in color, then flip with a spatula and cook the other side until golden and cooked through. Repeat with the remaining batter.	Serve with warm **maple syrup**.
apple-brie pancakes	In a large bowl, combine: ▸ 2 c. **unbleached all-purpose flour** ▸ 1 t. **baking powder** ▸ ½ t. **baking soda** ▸ ⅓ c. **sugar** ▸ A pinch of **salt** ▸ 1 t. **cinnamon**	To dry ingredients, add: ▸ 2 c. **buttermilk** ▸ 2 large **eggs**, lightly beaten ▸ 2 T. **unsalted butter**, melted ▸ 1 handful firm, chilled **brie**, rind removed, cut into small cubes. Stir all the ingredients together until they are just combined. It's okay if the batter is a bit lumpy. Don't overmix.	Heat your skillet or pan to medium-hot and brush it with a bit of butter. If a drop of water dropped onto the pan starts to dance, you are in the ballpark. Slowly pour about ⅓ c. of the batter onto the skillet. Place an extra-thin **apple** slice or two on top of the dollop of pancake batter as it is cooking. Wait until the pancake bottom is deep golden in color, then flip with a spatula and cook the other side until golden and cooked through. Repeat with the remaining batter and more apple slices.	Serve with crumbled **fake bacon**.
banana-macadamia pancakes	In a large bowl, combine: ▸ 2 c. **unbleached all-purpose flour** ▸ 1 t. **baking powder** ▸ ½ t. **baking soda** ▸ ⅓ c. **sugar** ▸ A pinch of **salt** ▸ 1 t. **nutmeg**, freshly grated	To dry ingredients, add: ▸ 2 c. **buttermilk** ▸ 2 large **eggs**, lightly beaten ▸ 2 T. **unsalted butter**, melted ▸ 1 big handful **sweetened shredded coconut** ▸ 1 big handful **macadamia nuts**, crushed Stir all the ingredients together until they are just combined. It's okay if the batter is a bit lumpy. Don't overmix.	Heat your skillet or pan to medium-hot and brush it with a bit of butter. If a drop of water dropped onto the pan starts to dance, you are in the ballpark. Slowly pour about ⅓ c. of the batter onto the skillet. Place about 3 extra-thin slices of **banana** on top of the dollop of pancake batter as it is cooking. Wait until the pancake bottom is deep golden in color, then flip with a spatula and cook the other side until golden and cooked through. Repeat with remaining batter and more banana slices. These take a bit longer to cook than most of the other pancakes in this book.	Top with sifted **powdered sugar**, **Pineapple Butter** (page 123), or crushed **honeycomb**.

STEP	1	2	3	4
TYPE OF PANCAKES	COMBINE DRY INGREDIENTS	ADD WET INGREDIENTS	COOK PANCAKES	FINISHING TOUCHES

berry-mascarpone pancakes	In a large bowl, combine:
	▸ 2 c. **unbleached all-purpose flour**
	▸ 1 t. **baking powder**
	▸ ½ t. **baking soda**
	▸ ⅓ c. **sugar**
	▸ A pinch of **salt**
		To dry ingredients, add:
		▸ 2 c. **buttermilk**
		▸ 2 large **eggs**, lightly beaten
		▸ 2 T. **unsalted butter**, melted
		▸ ⅓ c. **mascarpone**, lightly whisked with a fork
		Stir all the ingredients together until they are just combined.
			Heat your skillet or pan to medium-hot and brush it with a bit of butter. If a drop of water dropped onto the pan starts to dance, you are in the ballpark.
			   Slowly pour about ⅓ c. of the batter onto the skillet.
			   Sprinkle a few chopped **berries** on the dollop of pancake batter as it is cooking.
			   Wait until the pancake bottom is deep golden in color, then flip with a spatula and cook the other side until golden and cooked through. Repeat with remaining batter and more berries.
				Top with **Sweetened Fresh Whipped Cream** (page 16) or sifted **powdered sugar**.

lemon-poppy seed pancakes	In a large bowl, combine: ▸ 2 c. **unbleached all-purpose flour** ▸ 1 t. **baking powder** ▸ ½ t. **baking soda** ▸ ⅓ c. **sugar** ▸ A pinch of **salt**	To dry ingredients, add: ▸ 2 c. **buttermilk** ▸ 2 large **eggs**, lightly beaten ▸ 2 T. **unsalted butter**, melted ▸ ⅓ c. **poppy seeds** ▸ Grated zest of 4 **lemons** Stir all the ingredients together until they are just combined.	Heat your skillet or pan to medium-hot and brush it with a bit of butter. If a drop of water dropped onto the pan starts to dance, you are in the ballpark. Slowly pour about ⅓ c. of the batter onto the skillet. Wait until the pancake bottom is deep golden in color, then flip with a spatula and cook the other side until golden and cooked through. Repeat with remaining batter.	Top with **Sweetened Fresh Whipped Cream** (page 16) and fresh **berries**.
pumpkin-walnut pancakes	In a large bowl, combine ▸ 2 c. **unbleached all-purpose flour** ▸ 1 t. **baking powder** ▸ ½ t. **baking soda** ▸ ⅓ c. **sugar** ▸ A pinch of **salt** ▸ 1 t. **cinnamon** ▸ 1 t. freshly grated **nutmeg** ▸ A pinch of ground **cloves**.	To dry ingredients, add: ▸ 2 c. **buttermilk** ▸ 2 large **eggs**, lightly beaten ▸ 2 T. **unsalted butter**, melted ▸ ⅓ c. **pumpkin puree** ▸ 2 big handfuls **walnuts**, chopped Stir all the ingredients together until they are just combined.	Heat your skillet or pan to medium-hot and brush it with a bit of butter. If a drop of water dropped onto the pan starts to dance, you are in the ballpark. Slowly pour about ⅓ c. of the batter onto the skillet. Wait until the pancake bottom is deep golden in color, then flip with a spatula and cook the other side until golden and cooked through.	Top with **Sweetened Fresh Whipped Cream** (page 16).

MUSHROOM MEDLEY FRITTATA

frittatas

There must be a hundred different ways you can cook eggs – poach, scramble, fry, hard-cook, soft-cook, sunny side up, over easy, under easy – but I love frittatas the most. You can make them bite-sized or family style, and what you put in them is limited only by your imagination.

Think of a frittata as an open-faced Italian omelet. These recipes are flexible, tough to screw up, and the frittatas can be served hot, room temperature, or any temperature in between.

Don't think you're limited to having frittatas for breakfast; they're great for lunch or a picnic. A wedge of a tomato-filled frittata is wonderful with a bright mixed green salad, and you can even slice one up and make a frittata sandwich served between thin, toasted pieces of artisan bread that have been rubbed with a garlic clove.

CHOICE OF PAN I realize most people aren't going to run out and buy the perfect frittata-making pan, and you don't really need to. You can cook a frittata in anything from a cast-iron skillet to a state-of-the-art nonstick ovenproof sauté pan. Most people have something in between. If you have a well-seasoned cast-iron skillet, go ahead and use it. You can serve the frittata right out of the pan, so you don't need to worry as much about whether it's going to stick or not.

This recipe calls for a 450°F oven, which works well because your eggs firm up and get beautifully golden very quickly. Some people even finish off their frittatas in the broiler. Don't worry if you have a pan that's only ovenproof to 350°F. Just follow these recipes using a 350°F oven and cook the frittata for about 20 minutes. Don't overcook, or you'll end up with a dried-out frittata.

I'm sold on the slipperiness of nonstick pans for cooking eggs, but I also love the character of old cast-iron skillets. So play around and figure out what works for you, but don't be deterred from making a recipe because you don't have the perfect equipment. Use common sense, a close eye, and make sensible adjustments.

tips

- I like a little crunch with my frittata. Sprinkle it with bread crumbs before you put it in the oven, or sprinkle it with dark, crisp fried shallots as it comes out.

- Bite-sized frittatas are great for parties and fun for children. Lightly grease a nonstick mini muffin pan and spoon a bit of the frittata mixture into each cup. Bake at 450°F until golden and puffy, 5 to 6 minutes.

- It's important to finely chop any ingredients you intend to add to your frittata. They'll only have a few minutes to cook all the way through.

- Remember that the handle on your ovenproof skillet can stay hot long after you remove it from the oven, so be sure to use an oven mitt. I've learned this the hard way.

STEP	1	2	3
TYPE OF FRITTATA	GET EGGS READY	SAUTÉ + ASSEMBLE FRITTATA	BAKE + GARNISH
heirloom tomato frittata	*Preheat oven to 450°F. In a medium bowl, whisk together:* ▸ *6 large* **eggs** ▸ *A splash of* **cream** ▸ *A pinch of* **s+p** ▸ *½ c. grated* **Gruyère cheese** ▸ *1 c. small, very thinly sliced heirloom* **tomatoes** *(mixed colors look nice)* *Reserve a slice or two of tomato for garnish. Set aside.*	*To an 8½-inch ovenproof nonstick skillet over medium-high heat, add:* ▸ *1 T.* **olive oil** ▸ *1* **shallot**, *minced* ▸ *1 clove* **garlic**, *minced* *Sauté, stirring constantly, until the shallot starts to soften up and get a bit translucent, about 2 minutes. Turn down the heat a bit.* *Add the egg mixture and cook over medium-low heat for about 5 minutes, or until just set and there isn't a lot of liquid. Run a spatula underneath the sides of the frittata and tilt the pan so the uncooked eggs run to the underside and cook.*	*Place the skillet in the oven and bake for about 9 minutes, or until golden, firm, and puffy.* *Add a couple fresh slices of tomatoes and some slivered* **basil** *as garnish. A touch of grated* **lemon zest** *on top is tasty too.*
mushroom medley frittata	*Preheat oven to 450°F. In a medium bowl, whisk together:* ▸ *6 large* **eggs** ▸ *A splash of* **cream** ▸ *A pinch of both* **s+p** ▸ *½ c. freshly grated* **Parmesan cheese** *Set aside.*	*To an 8 ½-inch ovenproof nonstick skillet over medium-high heat, add:* ▸ *1 T.* **olive oil** ▸ *2* **shallots**, *thinly sliced* ▸ *1 clove* **garlic**, *minced* *Sauté, stirring constantly, until the shallots start to soften up and get a bit translucent, about 2 minutes.* *Stir in 1 c. thinly sliced* **mushrooms** *(I like to mix different types). Cook until the mushrooms release their liquid, about 5 minutes. Turn down the heat a bit.* *Add the egg mixture and cook over medium-low heat for about 5 minutes, or until just set and there isn't a lot of liquid. Run a spatula underneath the sides of the frittata and tilt the pan so the uncooked eggs run to the underside and cook.*	*Sprinkle with fresh* **bread crumbs** *(optional).* *Place the skillet in the oven and bake for about 9 minutes, or until golden, firm, and puffy.* *Garnish with a sprig of fresh* **lemon thyme**, *or a sprinkling of* **Parmesan cheese**.

STEP	1	2	3
TYPE OF FRITTATA	GET EGGS READY	SAUTÉ + ASSEMBLE FRITTATA	BAKE + GARNISH

spinach frittata	Preheat oven to 450°F. In a medium bowl, whisk together:
	▸ 6 large **eggs**
	▸ A splash of **cream**
	▸ A pinch of both **s+p**
	▸ ½ c. freshly grated **Parmesan cheese**
	▸ ⅓ c. **dried apricots**, chopped
	Set aside.
		To an 8½-inch ovenproof nonstick skillet over medium-high heat, add:
		▸ 1 T. **olive oil**
		▸ 1 **shallot**, minced
		▸ 1 clove **garlic**, minced
		Sauté, stirring constantly, until the shallot starts to soften up and get a bit translucent, about 2 minutes.
		   Stir in 2 generous handfuls rinsed **spinach** leaves. Cook until the spinach starts to wilt, 1 minute or so. Turn down the heat a bit.
		   Add the egg mixture and cook over medium-low heat for about 5 minutes, or until just set and there isn't a lot of liquid. Run a spatula underneath the sides of the frittata and tilt the pan so the uncooked eggs run to the underside and cook.
			Place the skillet in the oven and bake for about 9 minutes, or until golden, firm, and puffy.
			   Garnish with some crumbled **feta cheese** and toasted **pine nuts** (see page 16).

tri-color potato frittata	Preheat oven to 450°F. In a medium bowl, whisk together:
	▸ 6 large **eggs**
	▸ A splash of **cream**
	▸ A pinch of both **s+p**
	▸ ½ c. freshly grated **Parmesan cheese**
	▸ ½ c. crumbled **goat cheese**
	▸ 1 handful paper-thin slices of small **potatoes** (I like Yukon gold, red, and purple potatoes)
	Set aside.
		To an 8½-inch ovenproof nonstick skillet over medium-high heat, add:
		▸ 1 T. **olive oil**
		▸ 3 **shallots**, thinly sliced
		▸ 1 clove **garlic**, minced
		▸ 1½ t. **red-pepper flakes**
		Sauté, stirring constantly, until the shallots start to soften up and get a bit translucent, about 2 minutes. Turn down the heat a bit.
		   Add the egg mixture and cook over medium-low heat for about 5 minutes, or until just set and there isn't a lot of liquid. Run a spatula underneath the sides of the frittata and tilt the pan so the uncooked eggs run to the underside and cook.
			Place the skillet in the oven and bake for about 9 minutes, or until golden, firm, and puffy.
			   Add a crumble of **goat cheese** to the top in the final 2 minutes (optional).
			   Sprinkle 1 or 2 handfuls snipped fresh **chives** on top; slivered basil is great, too.

LUNCHBOX

panini / quesadillas /
pocket tarts / savory kabobs /
thin-crust pizzas

BRIE, APPLE-CRANBERRY + FAKE BACON PANINI

panini MAKES 1 SANDWICH

A good panini has the potential to change the way you think about sandwiches. Simply put, panini is a grilled Italian sandwich made on a structured bread and filled with delicious, simple, fresh ingredients. They are most often wide and thin, making them easy to eat. The crunch of a grilled crust followed by the oozy goodness of a warm filling is magical.

I like to make panini on my electric Italian sandwich grill, but they can just as easily be made on a standard stovetop by cooking them in a pan or skillet. Just smoosh them down by placing another heavy skillet on top of the panini as it's cooking. Flip once to cook both sides.

THE RIGHT FOUNDATION Panini need a good, strong foundation to build on: namely, the right bread. Typical fillings include melty cheeses, tapenades, and vegetables that can expel moisture as the sandwich heats up, so the standard sandwich bread that comes in a plastic bag with a twisty tie isn't going to cut it. You really want a bread that's able to soak up any flavorful juices without becoming soggy.

FAVORITE BREADS FOR PANINI

Ciabatta: Gets a nice crust going, isn't too tall, and has plenty of air pockets where cheese and fillings can hide.

Focaccia: Many of the same advantages as ciabatta, but not quite as structured. It is nice because you can now find foccacia in quite a few flavors like herb or sun-dried tomato. Focaccia is great for extra flavor, and readily available.

Sweet baguette: You can find sweet baguettes just about anywhere. They hold up nicely if you're wrapping panini for a picnic or a lunchbox.

tips

- When you're cooking your panini make sure the pan or grill isn't too hot. You don't want to burn the outside of the roll and have the insides still cold. A nice medium heat should give you a golden, crisp crust just as the insides are getting hot.

- Try tossing any greens you're using on your panini with a good homemade vinaigrette (see pages 130–133) before adding them to your sandwich.

- Rub the crust of savory panini with a peeled clove of garlic as it comes off the grill. It smells amazing, and adds a boost of flavor.

- Experiment and improvise with new ingredients. Keep an eye out for interesting tapenades, spreads, and chutneys to try on your panini.

STEP	1	2	3
TYPE OF PANINI	PREPARE BREAD	ASSEMBLE SANDWICH	GRILL + GARNISH
brie, apple-cranberry + fake bacon panini	1 *ciabatta roll*, split lengthwise	Spread a generous chunk of **brie** on the top and bottom of the roll. Rind or no rind is your preference – I go for no rind. Place about 10 very thin slices of **apple** on one half of the roll, and sprinkle 1 handful of **dried cranberries** on the other half, pressing them into the brie so they stick in the sandwich. Pan-fry 5 or 6 slices **fake bacon** according to package instructions and lay the crisp strips on top of the apples.	Put the two halves of the sandwich together and, using a sandwich press on medium, or a cast-iron griddle or skillet over medium heat, cook slowly until the crust is crisp and the insides are hot, about 6 minutes.
goat cheese + walnut panini	1 *ciabatta roll*, split lengthwise	Spread a generous chunk of **goat cheese** on the top and bottom of the roll. Don't worry if it's crumbly, just smoosh it gently onto the roll. Sprinkle 1 handful toasted **walnuts** (page 16) on one half of the roll, and 1 handful **golden raisins** on the other half. Drizzle 2 T. **honey** over the walnut half, with a quick shake of **s+p**.	Put the two halves of the sandwich together and, using a sandwich press on medium, or a cast-iron griddle or skillet over medium heat, cook slowly until the crust is crisp and the insides are hot, about 6 minutes. When the sandwich comes off the grill, let it cool for a minute, then carefully open it up and put 1 generous handful **mixed greens** inside the panini. Close it up again and enjoy.
marinated artichoke panini	⅓ or ½ *sweet baguette*, split lengthwise	Spread a generous chunk of **goat cheese** on both pieces of bread. Don't worry if it's crumbly, just smoosh it gently onto the bread. Place about ⅔ c. **marinated artichokes** on one half of the bread. Try to get them to lay relatively flat. Grate a generous dose of **Parmesan cheese** on top of the artichokes, and sprinkle the zest of 1 grated **lemon** on top of that. Finish with a good shake of **s+p**.	Put the two halves of the sandwich together and, using a sandwich press on medium, or a cast-iron griddle or skillet on medium heat, cook slowly until the crust is crisp and the insides are hot, about 6 minutes. When the sandwich comes off the grill, let it cool for a minute, then carefully open it up and put about 10 fresh **basil** leaves inside the panini. Close it up again and enjoy.

STEP	1	2	3
TYPE OF PANINI	PREPARE BREAD	ASSEMBLE SANDWICH	GRILL + GARNISH
panini margherita	1 *focaccia* or *ciabatta roll*, split lengthwise	*Drizzle 1 t. good-quality* **extra-virgin olive oil** *across the inside of both pieces of bread.* *On the bottom half of the bread, lay thin slices of fresh* **whole-milk mozzarella** *(or smash bocconcini balls between your fingers to flatten them out a bit).* *Cut a medium* **tomato** *into thin slices, and layer them on top of the cheese.* *Finish with a good shake of* **s+p** *and the grated zest of 1* **lemon**.	*Put the two halves of the sandwich together and, using a sandwich press on medium, or a cast-iron griddle or skillet over medium heat, cook slowly until the crust is crisp and the insides are hot, about 6 minutes.* *When the sandwich comes off the grill, let it cool for a minute, then carefully open it up and arrange about 10 or so fresh* **basil** *leaves (whole or slivered). Close it up again, rub the crust with a peeled* **garlic** *clove, and enjoy.*
PBJ + banana panini	2 slices sturdy white or 9-grain **bread**	*Spread a generous amount of* **jam** *or jelly on one slice of the bread. (I like using berry jams for this panini.) Spread a generous amount of chunky* **peanut butter** *on the other slice.* *Place thin slices of ripe* **banana** *on one half of the bread. Sprinkle with 1 T.* **brown sugar** *(optional).*	*Put the two halves of the sandwich together and, using a sandwich press on medium, or a cast-iron griddle or skillet over medium heat, cook slowly until the crust is crisp and the insides are hot, about 6 minutes.*
roasted vegetable panini	1 *focaccia* or *ciabatta roll*, split lengthwise	*Drizzle 1 t. good-quality* **extra-virgin olive oil** *across the inside of both pieces of bread.* *On the bottom half of the bread, spread a thin layer of* **Pesto Sauce** *(page 126). Add a few slices of fresh* **whole-milk mozzarella**. *Choose an assortment of* **Roasted Vegetables** *(pages 106–111) and add them to the sandwich. Finish with a good shake of* **s+p**.	*Put the two halves of the sandwich together and, using a sandwich press on medium, or a cast-iron griddle or skillet over medium heat, cook slowly until the crust is crisp and the insides are hot, about 6 minutes.* *When the sandwich comes off the grill, let it cool for a minute, then carefully open it up and put in 1 handful of fresh* **baby greens** *inside (optional). Close it up again and enjoy.*

quesadillas

The quesadilla was one of the first things I learned to make as a kid. Think of a quesadilla as a Mexican grilled cheese sandwich where the cheese and a variety of other fillings are sandwiched inside a tortilla, then cooked in a skillet, grilled, or baked.

I couldn't have been more than six or seven when my two cousins, who were a bit older and more worldly than my sister and me, showed us how to make quesadillas using my dad's electric crêpe/omelet pan. I think my parents thought that if it plugged into the wall, we were less likely to burn the house down. My sister Heather and I loved it when they would come to visit because in addition to quesadillas, they also turned us on to things like friendship pins, and eventually hair mousse.

Every day growing up I would pull up a chair (I wasn't tall enough to reach the counter on my own) and make quesadillas for us as an after-school snack. Of course, to my parents' dismay we refused to eat whole wheat tortillas – we would have only white tortillas with cheddar. Thankfully, things have evolved since then.

These days I usually make quesadillas on the stovetop and raid the fridge for good toppings – quick and easy. If I have a little extra time, I make homemade tortillas.

HOMEMADE TORTILLAS You should aim to make your own tortillas. It's easy, quick, and very much worth the effort. If you've never tried to make a homemade tortilla, this is your time. They completely transform a quesadilla or soft taco, and as far as simple foods go there are few things as good as a fresh, hot tortilla with a bit of good salsa and a shake of salt.

> 2 c. **unbleached all-purpose flour**
> 1 t. **baking powder**
> 1 t. **salt**
> 2 T. **vegetable shortening**
> ¾ c. warm **water**

In a food processor, combine the flour, baking powder, salt, and shortening. Pulse until the mixture resembles coarse meal. Transfer to a large bowl.

Stir in the warm water a bit at a time until a stiff dough forms – not sticky and not dry. Cut the dough into 8 or 12 pieces (depending on whether you are making small or large tortillas), and form each into a ball. Let the dough rest, covered with plastic wrap or a cloth, for at least 15 minutes.

Roll or flatten each piece of dough into a thin circle at least 6 inches across. Cook on an ungreased skillet or griddle over medium-high heat until barely golden, about 45 seconds on each side.

TOPPING IDEAS Try salsa, chives, sour cream (infused with different flavors), chiles, avocado, guacamole, herbs, green onions, or chopped grilled vegetables.

- *Taste and try different types of tortillas: corn, whole wheat, and flavored tortillas can add a variety of tastes and textures.*
- *Using the microwave oven for quesadillas should be avoided. You'll end up with a limp, soggy, steaming tortilla instead of a nice golden,* *crisp crust. You'll also miss out on the chance to get some of those dark, crisp morsels that happen when cheese trickles out of your tortilla onto a sizzling hot pan.*
- *Go easy on the cheese. I like to use cheese more as an accent than a base, for a more healthful quesadilla. I avoid* *ordering quesadillas in restaurants because, more often than not, I get a pound of cheese barely melted between two greasy tortillas. No one wants to eat that much cheese.*
- *For easy wedges, cut the quesadillas with a pizza cutter or scissors.*

STEP	1	2	3
TYPE OF QUESADILLA	CREATE FILLING	ASSEMBLE QUESADILLA	COOK + GARNISH
basic cheese quesadillas	In a medium bowl, gently toss together: ▸ 1 c. crumbled **queso fresco** ▸ 1 c. **Salsa Fresca** (page 128). Note: Queso fresco can be found in the refrigerated Mexican food section of many grocery stores. Monterey Jack cheese is a fine substitution, but it will have a different consistency and taste.	Place a skillet over medium-low heat. Run a stick of **butter** quickly across the bottom of the pan. Place one **tortilla** in the pan and add enough of the cheese mixture to create a thin layer across the bottom of the tortilla. Place another tortilla on top, forming a sandwich.	Cook the quesadilla until the bottom is golden brown. Flip, and cook the other side until browned – the second side always cooks faster. Use the remaining filling to make more quesadillas.
black olive quesadillas	In a medium bowl, gently toss together: ▸ ½ c. pitted **kalamata olives**, chopped ▸ 1 c. crumbled **queso fresco** (see Note above) ▸ 2 T. **Pesto Sauce** (page 126)	Place a skillet over medium-low heat. Run a stick of **butter** quickly across the bottom of the pan. Place one **tortilla** in the pan and add enough of the cheese mixture to create a thin layer across the bottom of the tortilla. Place another tortilla on top, forming a sandwich.	Cook the quesadilla until the bottom is golden brown. Flip, and cook the other side until browned – the second side always cooks faster. Use the remaining filling to make more quesadillas.

cinnamon-sugar quesadillas	In a medium bowl, gently toss together:
	▸ ⅓ c. **sugar**
	▸ 1 t. **cinnamon**
		Place a skillet over medium-low heat. Spread a generous layer of **mascarpone** across a white-flour **tortilla**. Sprinkle with a generous dose of the cinnamon sugar. Place another tortilla on top, forming a sandwich.
		    Run a stick of **butter** quickly across the bottom of the pan. Place the quesadilla in the pan.
			Cook the quesadilla until the bottom is golden brown. Flip, and cook the other side until browned. Be careful, though: The mascarpone can splatter a bit when being flipped. Use the remaining filling to make more quesadillas.
			    Great with vanilla ice cream.

smashed black bean quesadillas	In a medium bowl, gently toss together: ▸ 1 (15-oz.) can **black beans**, drained (smash the beans a bit against the side of the bowl) ▸ 1 c. **corn** kernels ▸ 1 **red bell pepper**, minced ▸ 1 **avocado**, cut into small cubes ▸ 1 c. crumbled **queso fresco** (see Note above) ▸ A squeeze of **lime juice**	Place a skillet over medium-low heat. Run a stick of **butter** quickly across the bottom of the pan. Place one **tortilla** in the pan and add enough of the cheese and bean mixture to create a thin layer across the bottom of the tortilla. Place another tortilla on top, forming a sandwich.	Cook the quesadilla until the bottom is golden brown. Flip, and cook the other side until browned – the second side always cooks faster. Use the remaining filling to make more quesadillas.

pocket tarts MAKES 9 (3½-INCH) TARTS

Pocket tarts are really cute and equally tasty. Similar in spirit to empanadas or calzones, these tarts are made using puff pastry and can be stuffed with an endless variety of fillings.

I call these pocket tarts because they're small enough to fit into a baggy pocket (although I'm not sure I recommend this). They are also the perfect size for a lunchbox or picnic lunch. Wrap them up in parchment paper, and they're terrific hot or cold.

To keep the method for these recipes short and sweet, we're going to use store-bought puff pastry, which works like a charm. It puffs up really nicely and gets billowy and golden. The fillings are all created by doing a quick sauté of ingredients to get everything nice and brown, seasoned, and precooked a bit before filling the tarts.

tips

- *Get a golden crust by brushing the tarts with a lightly beaten egg before placing them in the oven.*
- *Use mini cookie cutters to cut hearts, butterflies, stars, or initials from scraps of puff pastry and paste them to the tops of the tarts with a dab of egg wash. I like to add cutouts of little carrots or tomatoes to the tops of vegetarian pocket tarts.*

- *For mixed crowds, add a little fish or piglet cutout to the tops of nonvegetarian tarts to indicate the filling.*

INDIAN-SPICED POCKET TARTS

STEP	1	2	3
TYPE OF POCKET TART	CREATE FILLING	ASSEMBLE POCKET TART	BRUSH WITH EGG WASH + BAKE
indian-spiced pocket tarts	Preheat oven to 400°F. Heat a large skillet over medium-high heat. Add: ▸ 1 T. **ghee** or olive oil ▸ 3 cloves **garlic**, minced ▸ 1 ½ T. **garam masala** (Indian spice mix) Toast for 1 to 2 minutes, until the spices are fragrant. Stir in: ▸ 1 c. chopped **tomatoes** ▸ 1 (15-oz.) can **chickpeas**, drained ▸ A generous pinch of **salt** Cover and simmer 5 minutes.	Unwrap a 17-oz. box of **puff pastry dough** onto a lightly floured surface. Quickly run a rolling pin over the puff pastry only once or twice to make it a bit bigger and flatter. Using a 3-inch square cookie cutter, cut out 18 squares. Fill half of the squares with a spoonful of the filling. Place another square on top and gently press down on the edges to seal. Use the tines of a fork to press down on the edges the way you would a pie crust, to reinforce the seal and keep the filling from leaking.	Lightly beat 1 **egg** in a small bowl. Set aside. Place the tarts on a cookie sheet lined with parchment paper. Brush each tart with egg wash, then poke a few holes in the tops of the tarts to allow steam to escape. Bake on the middle rack of the oven for 15 minutes, or until the tarts are puffed and golden.
potato-leek pocket tarts	Preheat oven to 400°F. Heat a large skillet over medium-high heat. Add: ▸ 1 T. **extra-virgin olive oil** ▸ 4 cloves **garlic**, peeled ▸ 2 c. diced unpeeled **new potatoes** (¼-inch dice) ▸ 1 c. chopped **leeks**, white parts only Stirring occasionally, cook until the potatoes and leeks are golden and cooked through, about 10 minutes. Add **s+p** to taste. Crumble ½ c. **goat cheese** and set aside.	Unwrap a 17-oz. box of **puff pastry dough** onto a lightly floured surface. Quickly run a rolling pin over the puff pastry only once or twice to make it a bit bigger and flatter. Using a 3-inch square cookie cutter, cut out 18 squares. Fill half of the squares with a spoonful of the filling. Add a bit of goat cheese to each tart. Place another square on top and gently press down on the edges to seal. Use the tines of a fork to press down on the edges the way you would a pie crust, to reinforce the seal and keep the filling from leaking.	Lightly beat 1 **egg** in a small bowl. Set aside. Place the tarts on a cookie sheet lined with parchment paper. Brush each tart with egg wash, then poke a few holes in the tops of the tarts to allow steam to escape. Bake on the middle rack of the oven for 15 minutes, or until the tarts are puffed and golden.

STEP	1	2	3
TYPE OF POCKET TART	CREATE FILLING	ASSEMBLE POCKET TART	BRUSH WITH EGG WASH + BAKE
spinach pocket tarts	Preheat oven to 400°F. Heat a large skillet over medium-high heat. Add: ▸ 2 T. unsalted **butter** ▸ 2 **shallots**, chopped Sauté until the shallots are a bit soft. Add 10 handfuls roughly chopped rinsed **spinach**. Cook for 1 to 2 minutes, until the spinach shrinks and wilts. Stir in: ▸ 6 plump **dried apricots**, chopped ▸ ¼ c. toasted **pine nuts** (see page 16) ▸ 3 pinches **salt** ▸ ¼ c. freshly grated **Parmesan cheese**	Unwrap a 17-oz. box of **puff pastry dough** onto a lightly floured surface. Quickly run a rolling pin over the puff pastry only once or twice to make it a bit bigger and flatter. Using a 3-inch square cookie cutter, cut out 18 squares. Fill half of the squares with a spoonful of the filling. Place another square on top and gently press down on the edges to seal. Use the tines of a fork to press down on the edges the way you would a pie crust, to reinforce the seal and keep the filling from leaking.	Lightly beat 1 **egg** in a small bowl. Set aside. Place the tarts on a cookie sheet lined with parchment paper. Brush each tart with egg wash, then poke a few holes in the tops of the tarts to allow steam to escape. Bake on the middle rack of the oven for 15 minutes, or until the tarts are puffed and golden.
tomato pocket tarts	Preheat oven to 400°F. In a medium bowl, gently toss together: ▸ 1 T. **extra-virgin olive oil** ▸ 2 c. diced and drained **tomatoes** ▸ ¼ c. pitted **kalamata olives**, chopped ▸ ⅔ c. chopped fresh **whole-milk mozzarella** Add **s+p** to taste.	Unwrap a 17-oz. box of **puff pastry dough** onto a lightly floured surface. Quickly run a rolling pin over the puff pastry only once or twice to make it a bit bigger and flatter. Using a 3-inch square cookie cutter, cut out 18 squares. Spread a touch of **Dijon mustard** on half of the squares and add a spoonful of the tomato filling. Place another square on top and gently press down on the edges to seal. Use the tines of a fork to press down on the edges the way you would a pie crust, to reinforce the seal and keep the filling from leaking.	Lightly beat 1 **egg** in a small bowl. Set aside. Place the tarts on a cookie sheet lined with parchment paper. Brush each tart with egg wash, then poke a few holes in the tops of the tarts to allow steam to escape. Bake on the middle rack of the oven for 15 minutes, or until the tarts are puffed and golden.

STEP	1	2	3
TYPE OF POCKET TART	CREATE FILLING	ASSEMBLE POCKET TART	BRUSH WITH EGG WASH + BAKE
wild mushroom pocket tarts	Preheat oven to 400°F. Heat a large skillet over medium-high heat. Add: ▸ 1 T. *extra-virgin olive oil* ▸ 2 *shallots*, chopped ▸ 1 clove *garlic*, chopped ▸ 3 c. chopped *shiitake*, *morel*, or *porcini mushrooms* Sauté for 3 minutes, or until the mushrooms release their liquid. Stir in: ▸ ½ c. *white wine* ▸ A pinch or two of fresh *thyme* Remove from the heat and stir in: ▸ ½ c. freshly grated *Parmesan cheese* ▸ *s+p*, add to taste.	Unwrap a 17-oz. box of **puff pastry dough** onto a lightly floured surface. Quickly run a rolling pin over the puff pastry only once or twice to make it a bit bigger and flatter. Using a 3-inch square cookie cutter, cut out 18 squares. Fill half of the squares with a spoonful of the filling. Place another square on top and gently press down on the edges to seal. Use the tines of a fork to press down on the edges the way you would a pie crust, to reinforce the seal and keep the filling from leaking.	Lightly beat 1 **egg** in a small bowl. Set aside. Place the tarts on a cookie sheet lined with parchment paper. Brush each tart with egg wash, then poke a few holes in the tops of the tarts to allow steam to escape. Bake on the middle rack of the oven for 15 minutes, or until the tarts are puffed and golden.
zucchini pocket tarts	Preheat oven to 400°F. Heat a large skillet over medium-high heat. Add: ▸ 1 T. *extra-virgin olive oil* ▸ 2 *shallots*, chopped ▸ 2 c. diced *zucchini* or other summer squash Stirring occasionally, cook until golden and cooked through, about 7 minutes. Stir in the grated zest of 1 *lemon*.	Unwrap a 17-oz. box of **puff pastry dough** onto a lightly floured surface. Quickly run a rolling pin over the puff pastry only once or twice to make it a bit bigger and flatter. Using a 3-inch square cookie cutter, cut out 18 squares. Fill half of the squares with a spoonful of the filling. Place another square on top and gently press down on the edges to seal. Use the tines of a fork to press down on the edges the way you would a pie crust, to reinforce the seal and keep the filling from leaking.	Lightly beat 1 **egg** in a small bowl. Set aside. Place the tarts on a cookie sheet lined with parchment paper. Brush each tart with egg wash, then poke a few holes in the tops of the tarts to allow steam to escape. Bake on the middle rack of the oven for 15 minutes, or until the tarts are puffed and golden.

savory kabobs

What could be more fun than a meal on a stick? Big kabobs can easily make a meal, and tiny ones make great snacks and party treats. We make kabobs all the time during the summer. Fire up the grill, invite a few close friends over, and sit out on the deck under the stars enjoying each other's company and eating the kabobs as they come off the grill.

I prefer to grill kabobs outdoors, but when bad weather rolls around or we run out of propane, I just throw them in the oven. They go well with all sorts of sides, especially with a fresh salad or risotto (pages 84-87).

GREAT THINGS TO SKEWER AND THROW ON THE GRILL
Try grilling bananas, disks of corn on the cob, pineapple, red onions, red peppers, whole white or cremini mushrooms, small potatoes, winter squash, summer squash, cherry tomatoes, onions (big and small), whole shallots, or whole garlic cloves.

DIFFERENT TYPES OF SKEWERS
Rosemary: Sturdy, and smells wonderful. Soak the sprigs in water before using.
Lemongrass: Nice for mini skewers. Slice on an angle to make a point. Soak in water before using.
Wood/Bamboo: Easy to find, wood skewers come in a variety of sizes. Popsicle sticks make good skewers for kids (no pointy edges). Soak them in water before using.
Metal: Reusable, and sturdy. Stainless-steel nonstick skewers are great — no rust, and the juices and food won't cling.

tips

- *I typically use Soy Deli firm Nigari tofu, although there are several good brands. Don't use the kind of tofu that is swimming in liquid; it will fall right off the skewer.*
- *Anything going on a skewer should be similar in shape and size. You don't want your mushrooms to cook in 5 minutes while your onions take an hour.*
- *Soak the bamboo skewers in water for a few minutes before loading them up and putting them on the grill. This helps keep your skewers from burning.*

- *Metal skewers are great for kabobs that include segments of corn. The metal skewers often have sharp ends that can pierce the tough cob of the corn, which can be a bit of a challenge when using bamboo. Be careful you don't stab yourself.*
- *If grilling isn't an option, just throw the kabobs on a baking sheet and place them in a 400°F oven, rotating every 5 minutes or so, until the kabobs are cooked through. Check for doneness regularly; cooking times will vary depending on the ingredients.*

- *Keep a close eye on the kabobs while they're cooking. If you're using an oven and the outsides of your kabobs are getting too dark and the insides aren't yet cooked, move them down to a lower rack and turn down the oven temperature a bit.*

STEP	1	2	3
TYPE OF KABOB	MARINATE	PREP + ASSEMBLE KABOBS	GRILL
simple kabobs	In a small bowl, whisk together: ▸ ½ c. *extra-virgin olive oil* ▸ ¼ c. *balsamic vinegar* ▸ 2 cloves *garlic*, minced ▸ A generous dose of *s+p* Cut 1 (12-oz.) package extra-firm *tofu* into 1-inch cubes. Shoot for about 18 cubes. Place everything in a resealable plastic bag and let marinate in the refrigerator for at least 1 hour or up to 1 day.	Cut 2 medium *red onions* into 8 wedges each. Rinse or brush the dirt off: ▸ 12 *cherry tomatoes* ▸ 12 whole *white* or *cremini mushrooms* Onto 6 medium-length soaked wood or metal skewers, alternately thread: 1 drained tofu cube, 1 mushroom, 1 red onion wedge, and 1 cherry tomato. Repeat.	Preheat grill to medium-high. You should be able to hold your hand over the grill for 2 to 3 seconds but no longer. Place the kabobs on the grill. Twirl and rotate regularly to make sure all sides get cooked. Brush every few minutes with leftover marinade. The kabobs are done when the vegetables are cooked through and the outsides are a bit crisp, about 25 minutes.
butternut squash kabobs	No marinade is needed, but you can brush the squash with *olive oil* as it is grilling.	Cut 1 *butternut squash* widthwise into 1-inch disks. Lay each disk flat and cut off any skin, seeds, or membranes. Cut the disks into 1-inch cubes. Onto 6 medium-length soaked wood or metal skewers, thread the squash cubes.	Preheat grill to medium. You should be able to hold your hand over the grill for 4 to 5 seconds but no longer. Place the kabobs on the grill and brush them with a bit of olive oil. Give them a good shake of *s+p* and a dash of *cayenne pepper*. Twirl and rotate regularly to make sure all sides get cooked. The kabobs are done when the squash is cooked through and the outsides are golden and caramelized, about 40 minutes. (Squash takes a long time to cook, and you don't want the outsides to burn while the insides are still raw.) To serve, drizzle with *Lime-Cilantro Vinaigrette* (page 132). These kabobs are also great with Black Bean Chowder (page 100).

STEP	1	2	3
TYPE OF KABOB	MARINATE	PREP + ASSEMBLE KABOBS	GRILL
mushroom kabobs	No marinade is needed, but you can brush the kabobs with **olive oil** as they are grilling.	Cut 2 medium **red onions** into eight wedges each. Brush the dirt off: ► 12 **white mushrooms** ► 12 **cremini mushrooms**. (Play around with different types of mushrooms.) Onto each of 6 medium-length soaked wood or metal skewers, alternately thread: 1 whole peeled **shallot**, 2 mushrooms, 1 red onion wedge, 2 mushrooms. Repeat.	Preheat grill to medium-high. You should be able to hold your hand over the grill for 2 to 3 seconds but no longer. Place the kabobs on the grill and brush them with a bit of olive oil. Give them a good shake of **s+p**. Twirl and rotate regularly to make sure all sides get cooked. The kabobs are done when the vegetables are cooked through and the outsides are a bit crisp, about 20 minutes. These are great served with **Herb Garden Risotto** (page 87).
red pepper + lemon kabobs	In a small bowl, whisk together: ► ½ c. **extra-virgin olive oil** ► ¼ c. fresh **lemon juice** (about 2 lemons) ► 2 T. **sugar** ► 2 cloves **garlic**, minced ► 1 t. **paprika** ► ½ t. **cayenne pepper** ► A few pinches of **salt** Cut 1 (12-oz.) package extra-firm **tofu** into 1-inch cubes. Shoot for about 18 cubes. Place everything in a resealable plastic bag and let marinate in the refrigerator for at least 1 hour or up to 1 day.	Cut 3 **lemons** in half lengthwise, then into 6 wedges. Cut 3 **red bell peppers** into 1-inch squares. Remove veins and seeds. Onto 6 medium-length soaked wood or metal skewers, alternately thread: 1 lemon wedge, 1 pepper square, 1 tofu cube, and another 1 pepper square. Repeat.	Preheat grill to medium-high. You should be able to hold your hand over the grill for 2 to 3 seconds but no longer. Place the kabobs on the grill. Twirl and rotate regularly to make sure all sides get cooked. Brush every few minutes with leftover marinade, reserving some of the marinade for serving. The kabobs are done when the vegetables are cooked through and the outsides are a bit crisp, about 25 minutes. Sprinkle with whole or slivered fresh **mint** leaves. Drizzle with reserved marinade.

STEP	1	2	3
TYPE OF KABOB	MARINATE	PREP + ASSEMBLE KABOBS	GRILL
smoky corn kabobs	In a small bowl, whisk together: ▸ ½ c. **extra-virgin olive oil** ▸ 3 T. **adobo sauce** from a can of chipotle chiles ▸ 1 T. **sugar** ▸ 2 cloves **garlic**, minced ▸ A pinch of **salt** Cut 1 (12-oz.) package extra-firm **tofu** into 1-inch cubes. Shoot for about 18 cubes. Place everything in a resealable plastic bag and let marinate in the refrigerator for at least 1 hour or up to 1 day.	Husk 2 ears of **corn** and cut into 1½-inch-wide disks. Then cut each disk into a half-circle. Cut about 10 small **red potatoes** in half. Onto 6 medium-length soaked wood or metal skewers, alternately thread: 1 potato half, 1 tofu cube, and 1 corn piece (see Note). Repeat. <u>Note</u>: Getting corn on the skewer can be a challenge. I skewer them where the kernels meet the cob, instead of through the tough center core of the cob itself.	Preheat grill to medium. You should be able to hold your hand over the grill for 4 to 5 seconds and no longer. Place the kabobs on the grill and cover. Rotate and twirl regularly to make sure all sides get cooked. Brush every few minutes with leftover marinade, reserving some of the marinade for serving. The kabobs are done when the potatoes are cooked through and the outsides of the tofu are a bit crisp, about 40 minutes. Sprinkle with chopped fresh **cilantro** (optional) and drizzle with the reserved marinade. These are great served with Rustic Potato Chowder (page 100).
spicy hawaiian kabobs	In a small bowl, whisk together: ▸ ⅓ c. **extra-virgin olive oil** ▸ ⅓ c. **pineapple juice** ▸ Grated zest and juice of 1 **lemon** ▸ ½ **habanero chile**, minced (hot!) ▸ 2 T. **honey** ▸ 1 (1-inch) piece **ginger**, peeled and grated ▸ A pinch of **salt** Cut 1 (12-oz.) package extra-firm **tofu** into 1-inch cubes. Shoot for about 18 cubes. Place everything in a resealable plastic bag and let marinate in the refrigerator for at least 1 hour or up to 1 day.	Cut 2 medium **red onions** into 6 or 8 wedges each. Core 1 medium **pineapple** and cut into 1-inch pieces (about 3 c.). Onto 6 medium-length soaked wood or metal skewers, alternately thread: 1 tofu cube, 1 pineapple cube, and 1 red onion wedge. Repeat.	Preheat grill to medium-high. You should be able to hold your hand over the grill for 2 to 3 seconds but no longer. Place the kabobs on the grill. Rotate and twirl regularly to make sure all sides get cooked. Brush every few minutes with leftover marinade. The kabobs are done when the onions are cooked through and the outsides of the tofu are a bit crisp, about 30 minutes. Serve sprinkled with chopped salted **macadamia nuts**.

thin-crust pizzas MAKES DOUGH FOR 6 INDIVIDUAL PIZZAS

Thin crust, thick crust, deep dish, New York style, Chicago style – everyone has an opinion about what makes a great pizza. There are only a couple ways you can go wrong with pizza: with the dough or with the quantity, quality, or combination of toppings.

There are a couple ways to go about making pizzas at home. Many people buy the premade crusts, a few of my friends hit up their favorite local pizzeria for dough, or, my favorite choice, you can make your own. Creating and using fresh dough makes all the difference in the world for your pizza. If you make a batch once every other weekend, you have pizza dough on hand for lunch, dinner, and snacks. Make-your-own pizza parties are a blast. You can set up a pizza bar with lots of toppings and invite a few friends over.

To make great pizzas you need to have a batch of dough ready. I've included my favorite everyday pizza dough recipe here. When it comes to toppings, I use the freshest ingredients I can get my hands on. I also use them sparingly; if you use a light hand with your toppings you won't weigh down your crust. In the end you should have a wonderful pizza with a deep, irregular, golden, slightly crunchy crust.

tips

- *Working with semisticky pizza dough takes a bit of practice and patience. There are a few tricks. If the dough doesn't seem to want to stretch, or keeps shrinking, you may have overworked it. Just let it rest while you make the next pizza.*

- *Resist the urge to use a rolling pin when you are shaping your pizza crust. You will get a much nicer rustic texture by pulling the dough into shape with your hands.*

- *Don't feel bad if your pizzas aren't perfectly round. Mine rarely are. If you tear a hole in your dough while you're pulling it out, your dough is a shade too thin – just patch it up by pinching the edges of the hole together and keep going.*

- *Don't let your pizza stick to the baking sheet. Evenly dust the bottom of your baking sheet with a thin layer of cornmeal. It makes a nice crunchy crust and helps get the pizza off the pan and onto a pizza stone, if you're using one.*

- *Pizza stones are the way to go. Combined with a nice hot oven, these stones help you get that nice thin, crisp crust. Authentico!*

- *I always drizzle a few drops of extra-virgin olive oil on my pizza right after it comes out of the hot oven.*

ONE-HOUR THIN-CRUST CORNMEAL PIZZA DOUGH

This makes enough dough for 6 pizzas. The dough is quick, easy, and forgiving. It makes one of my all-time favorite pizza crusts – thin, textured, delicious, and sturdy enough that it doesn't get soggy in the oven when the toppings start to heat up. The dough should be a bit on the sticky side. If you aren't going to use it immediately after it rises, just store it in the refrigerator. Take it out an hour before using it so it's at room temperature when you try to stretch it out.

If you don't like cornmeal in your pizza dough, just substitute an equivalent amount of flour.

4 1/4 c. **unbleached all-purpose flour**
1/2 c. **cornmeal** (or substitute 1/2 c. flour or a bit more)
1 1/2 t. **active dry yeast**
1 1/2 t. **salt**
1/4 c. **extra-virgin olive oil**
1 3/4 c. warm **water** (not hot)

In a large bowl or the bowl of an electric mixer, combine the flour, cornmeal, yeast, and salt. Add the oil and water. Mix slowly with dough hook attachment until the dough comes together, and then mix vigorously on medium-high speed for about 5 minutes. The dough should stick to the bottom of the bowl as you are mixing, but needs to come away from the sides (think of a tornado). If mixing by hand, knead the dough until you get tired or 10 minutes, whichever comes first. Finished dough should look smooth and elastic, but feel a bit tacky. Don't be afraid to beat it up a bit. If the dough is a bit too sticky, add a little flour. If it's too dry, add water just a dab at a time.

Form the dough into a big ball and rub it with a bit of oil. Place it in a large bowl in a warm place covered to rise for 1 hour. (I turn on my oven and place my rising dough on top of the stove). Punch down the dough when it has doubled in size, and pull it out of the bowl. Place it on a lightly floured counter.

Cut the dough in half, and then each half into thirds. You should have 6 pieces total. Gently form each piece into a small ball and rub each with a dab of oil. Proceed with the following recipes.

Place the dough you aren't going to use immediately into a freezer-proof plastic bag for future use. At this point it can go in the freezer for three months or the refrigerator for up to 3 days. Take the dough out of the refrigerator about 1 hour before you want to stretch it out and shape it. Let frozen dough thaw overnight in the refrigerator before using.

STEP	1	2	3
TYPE OF PIZZA	SHAPE PIZZA DOUGH	ADD A THIN LAYER OF TOPPINGS	PLACE PIZZA IN OVEN + BAKE
simple pizza margherita	Preheat oven (and a baking stone if you have one) to 450°F for at least 30 minutes. Gently pat **pizza dough** with a bit of flour. With your fingers and knuckles, gently pull the dough into an extra-thin round, ⅛ to ¼ inch thick and 7 to 8 inches wide. Place on a baking sheet dusted with **cornmeal**.	Brush the dough lightly with **extra-virgin olive oil**. Brush a thin layer of **Bright Red Tomato Sauce** (page 126) onto the dough, about ¼ c. Sprinkle with a pinch of **red-pepper flakes**. Add about ⅓ c. fresh **whole-milk mozzarella**; tear off about 15 smallish chunks and sprinkle them across the dough.	Slide the pizza onto the baking stone (or leave on the baking sheet). Bake for about 8 minutes, or until the crust is deeply golden but the toppings aren't burnt. Sprinkle with some fresh **basil** leaves and drizzle with a little extra-virgin olive oil when the pizza comes out of the oven.
feta + mint pizza	Preheat oven (and a baking stone if you have one) to 450°F for at least 30 minutes. Gently pat **pizza dough** with a bit of flour. With your fingers and knuckles, gently pull the dough into an extra-thin round, ⅛ to ¼ inch thick and 7 to 8 inches wide. Place on a baking sheet dusted with **cornmeal**.	Brush the dough lightly with **extra-virgin olive oil**. Grate a layer of **Parmesan cheese** onto the dough. Add ⅓ c. crumbled **feta cheese**.	Slide the pizza onto the baking stone (or leave on the baking sheet). Bake for about 8 minutes, or until the crust is deeply golden but the toppings aren't burnt. Sprinkle a bit of slivered fresh **mint** on top when pizza comes out of the oven.
fig, arugula + goat cheese pizza	Preheat oven (and a baking stone if you have one) to 450°F for at least 30 minutes. Gently pat **pizza dough** with a bit of flour. With your fingers and knuckles, gently pull the dough into an extra-thin round, ⅛ to ¼ inch thick and 7 to 8 inches wide. Place on a baking sheet dusted with **cornmeal**.	Brush the dough lightly with **extra-virgin olive oil**. Sprinkle a layer of crumbled **goat cheese** onto the dough, about ⅓ c. Add 1 fresh **fig**, stemmed and thinly sliced.	Slide the pizza onto the baking stone (or leave on the baking sheet). Bake for about 8 minutes, or until the crust is deeply golden but the toppings aren't burnt. Toss 1 generous handful of rinsed and dried **arugula** on top when pizza comes out of the oven.

STEP	1	2	3
TYPE OF PIZZA	SHAPE PIZZA DOUGH	ADD A THIN LAYER OF TOPPINGS	PLACE PIZZA IN OVEN + BAKE
new potato + pesto pizza	Preheat oven (and a baking stone if you have one) to 450°F for at least 30 minutes. Gently pat **pizza dough** with a bit of flour. With your fingers and knuckles, gently pull the dough into an extra-thin round, ⅛- to ¼-inch thick and 7 to 8 inches wide. Place on a baking sheet dusted with **cornmeal**.	Brush 2 T. room-temperature **Pesto Sauce** (page 126) onto the dough. Add about ⅓ c. fresh **whole-milk mozzarella**; tear off about 15 smallish chunks and sprinkle them across the dough. Add a few very thin slices from a small **new potato**. (I like to mix red, yellow, and purple potatoes.)	Slide the pizza onto the baking stone (or leave on the baking sheet). Bake for about 8 minutes, or until the crust is deeply golden but the toppings aren't burnt. Shave some **Parmesan cheese** on top and drizzle with a little **extra-virgin olive oil** as the pizza comes out of the oven.
pizza bianco	Preheat oven (and a baking stone if you have one) to 450°F for at least 30 minutes. Gently pat **pizza dough** with a bit of flour. With your fingers and knuckles, gently pull the dough into an extra-thin round, ⅛- to ¼-inch thick and 7 to 8 inches wide. Place on a baking sheet dusted with **cornmeal**.	Brush the dough lightly with **extra-virgin olive oil**. Grate a layer of **Parmesan cheese** onto the dough. Sprinkle with a few cloves of **garlic**, peeled and smashed. Add about ⅓ c. fresh **whole-milk mozzarella**; tear off about 15 smallish chunks and sprinkle them across the dough.	Slide the pizza onto the baking stone (or leave on the baking sheet). Bake for about 8 minutes, or until the crust is deeply golden but the toppings aren't burnt. Sprinkle 1 small handful of slivered fresh **basil** on top when pizza comes out of the oven.
pizza verde	Preheat oven (and a baking stone if you have one) to 450°F for at least 30 minutes. Gently pat **pizza dough** with a bit of flour. With your fingers and knuckles, gently pull the dough into an extra-thin round, ⅛- to ¼-inch thick and 7 to 8 inches wide. Place on a baking sheet dusted with **cornmeal**.	Brush 2 T. room temperature **Pesto Sauce** (page 126) onto the dough. Grate a thin layer of **Parmesan cheese** onto the dough. Crumble ¼ c. **goat cheese** on top. Add 2 small handfuls thin 1-inch **asparagus** pieces.	Slide the pizza onto the baking stone (or leave on the baking sheet). Bake for about 8 minutes, or until the crust is deeply golden but the toppings aren't burnt. Sprinkle with fresh chopped **chives** when pizza comes out of the oven.

STEP	1	2	3
TYPE OF PIZZA	SHAPE PIZZA DOUGH	ADD A THIN LAYER OF TOPPINGS	PLACE PIZZA IN OVEN + BAKE
pumpkin, mint + ricotta pizza	*Preheat oven (and a baking stone if you have one) to 450°F for at least 30 minutes.* *Gently pat **pizza dough** with a bit of flour. With your fingers and knuckles, gently pull the dough into an extra-thin round, ⅛- to ¼-inch thick and 7 to 8 inches wide.* *Place on a baking sheet dusted with **cornmeal**.*	*Gently spread ¼ c. **ricotta** onto the dough (fresh ricotta is best).* *Grate ⅓ c. fresh **pumpkin** flesh on top.* *Add a shake of **salt** and a bit of grated **lemon zest**.*	*Slide the pizza onto the baking stone (or leave on the baking sheet). Bake for about 8 minutes, or until the crust is deeply golden but the toppings aren't burnt.* *Sprinkle with slivered fresh **mint** and a generous grating of **Parmesan cheese** when pizza comes out of the oven.*
red pepper + olive pizza	*Preheat oven (and a baking stone if you have one) to 450°F for at least 30 minutes.* *Gently pat **pizza dough** with a bit of flour. With your fingers and knuckles, gently pull the dough into an extra-thin round, ⅛- to ¼-inch thick and 7 to 8 inches wide.* *Place on a baking sheet dusted with **cornmeal**.*	*Brush a thin layer of **Red Pepper Sauce** (page 126) onto the dough, about ¼ c.* *Add about ⅓ c. fresh **whole-milk mozzarella**; tear off about 15 smallish chunks and sprinkle them across the dough.* *Add a few pitted **kalamata olives**, torn into quarters.*	*Slide the pizza onto the baking stone (or leave on the baking sheet). Bake for about 8 minutes, or until the crust is deeply golden but the toppings aren't burnt.*
toasted nuts + olive pizza	*Preheat oven (and a baking stone if you have one) to 450°F for at least 30 minutes.* *Gently pat **pizza dough** with a bit of flour. With your fingers and knuckles, gently pull the dough into an extra-thin round, ⅛- to ¼-inch thick and 7 to 8 inches wide.* *Place on a baking sheet dusted with **cornmeal**.*	*Brush the dough lightly with **extra-virgin olive oil**.* *Brush ¼ c. **Bright Red Tomato Sauce** (page 126) onto the dough.* *Add about ⅓ c. fresh **whole-milk mozzarella**; tear off about 15 smallish chunks and sprinkle them across the dough.* *Add 1 small handful toasted **pine nuts** (see page 16). Add a medley of pitted fresh **olives**, green and black, torn into pieces.*	*Slide the pizza onto the baking stone (or leave on the baking sheet). Bake for about 8 minutes, or until the crust is deeply golden but the toppings aren't burnt.*

ONE-DISH DINNERS

pot pies / rice bowls / fondues / stir-fries /

pasta dishes / risottos

pot pies MAKES 4 TO 6 POT PIES

Pot pies might be my favorite kind of pie. They are warm, filling, savory, and endlessly adaptable. Paired with a small, simple green salad and a glass of wine, a pot pie is a tasty way to spend a winter evening – or any evening.

A fun thing to do is to throw a pot pie party. Invite a handful of friends and family over to assemble pies and have everyone bring a different filling. Hang out in the kitchen, assembling your pies; pop a few in the oven to eat immediately, and throw the rest in the freezer until people are ready to go home. At the end of the party everyone takes home plenty of pot pies in different flavors. As host you can provide the crusts and beverages.

Of course, the big trick is remembering what fillings are in which pies. Sometimes my dad will make a chicken pot pie filling while I whip up a vegetarian filling. Similar to the Pocket Tarts (pages 47-50), I like to top the nonvegetarian pies with a pastry cutout of a chicken, and the veggie pies with a pastry cutout of a carrot or tomato shape. If people want a quick way to remember which ones are theirs, just use a cookie cutter to cut out the initials of each person from leftover pastry scraps. There's lots of fun to be had on the tops of these pies.

For simplicity's sake, we're going to go with a puff pastry dough for the pie lids. Feel free to experiment with other doughs as well. A few dollops of the Basic Drop Biscuit dough (page 28) is also great in place of the puff pastry or a standard pie crust. Cook biscuit-topped pies at 400°F until the biscuit is golden and the filling is bubbling.

tips

- *Thick and hearty soups or stews make great fillings. Use any of the chowder recipes (pages 98–101) or your own favorite chunky soup as fillings.*
- *Make sure your filling is well seasoned before baking; it's hard to season a pot pie after you've put the crust on.*

- *Freeze any extra filling you have. Assembling the already-made filling and puff pastry top takes less than 5 minutes. Just thaw the filling out in the refrigerator the day you want to make the pies, and pull out the puff pastry a half hour before you want to bake. Same deal using a biscuit topping.*
- *Resist the urge to use large bowls for these pot pies. Small to medium-sized bowls that aren't deeper than they are wide work best.*

- *Place a baking sheet under your pot pies in the oven, in case they start to bubble over a bit. This way they won't spatter all over your oven.*

STEP	1	2	3
TYPE OF POT PIE	START PIE FILLING	ADD MAIN INGREDIENT, LIQUID + SEASONING	POUR INTO BOWL + BAKE
chipotle-potato pot pie	*Preheat oven to 400°F.* *To a large pot over medium-high heat, add:* ▸ *3 T. **extra-virgin olive oil*** ▸ *1 **onion**, chopped* ▸ *3 cloves **garlic**, chopped* ▸ *2 c. diced **potatoes** (¼-inch dice)* ▸ *½ t. **salt*** *Sauté, stirring occasionally, for about 10 minutes, or until the potatoes are tender.*	*Stir in:* ▸ *1 T. **adobo sauce** from a can of chipotle chiles* ▸ *1 c. **corn** kernels* *In a small bowl, combine:* ▸ *2 c. cold **milk*** ▸ *2 T. **cornstarch*** *Stir into the potato mixture. Bring to a boil, stirring constantly, and cook until the filling starts to thicken.* *Remove from the heat and season with more salt to taste.*	*Pour the filling into small ovenproof bowls, each three quarters full.* *Cut a piece of **puff pastry dough** to fit each bowl, with some overlap. Place the dough on the bowls and fold over the edges. Brush the dough lightly with **egg white** for a golden crust. Poke a few holes in the top with a fork to allow steam to escape.* *Bake until the crusts are tall and deeply golden, about 15 minutes.*
creamy mushroom pot pie	*Preheat oven to 400°F.* *To a large pot over medium-high, heat add:* ▸ *3 T. **extra-virgin olive oil*** ▸ *1 **onion**, chopped* ▸ *3 **shallots**, chopped* ▸ *4 cloves **garlic**, chopped* ▸ *6 c. sliced **mushrooms*** ▸ *A pinch of fresh **tarragon*** *Sauté, stirring occasionally, for 7 to 10 minutes, until the mushrooms give up their liquid.*	*Stir in:* ▸ *½ t. **salt*** ▸ *¼ t. **pepper*** ▸ *¼ c. **dry sherry*** *In a small bowl, combine:* ▸ *2 c. cold **milk*** ▸ *2 T. **cornstarch*** *Pour into the mushroom mixture. Bring to a boil, stirring constantly, and cook until the filling starts to thicken.* *Remove from the heat and season with more **s+p** to taste.*	*Pour the filling into small ovenproof bowls, each three quarters full.* *Cut a piece of **puff pastry dough** to fit each bowl, with some overlap. Place the dough on the bowls and fold over the edges. Brush the dough lightly with **egg white** for a golden crust. Poke a few holes in the top with a fork to allow steam to escape.* *Bake until the crusts are tall and deeply golden, about 15 minutes.*
fall vegetable pot pie	*Preheat oven to 400°F.* *To a large pot over medium-high, add:* ▸ *3 T. **extra-virgin olive oil*** ▸ *3 **shallots**, chopped* ▸ *2 cloves **garlic**, chopped* ▸ *1 bulb **fennel**, chopped* ▸ *½ t. **salt*** *Sauté, stirring frequently, for about 3 minutes.*	*Stir in:* ▸ *4 c. diced **butternut squash** (¼-inch dice)* *Sauté for about 15 minutes, or until the squash is tender and cooked.* *In a small bowl, combine:* ▸ *2 c. **milk*** ▸ *2 T. **cornstarch*** *Pour into the vegetable mixture. Bring to a boil, stirring constantly, and cook until the filling starts to thicken.* *Remove from the heat.*	*Pour the filling into small ovenproof bowls, each three quarters full.* *Cut a piece of **puff pastry dough** to fit each bowl, with some overlap. Place the dough on the bowls and fold over the edges. Brush the dough lightly with **egg white** for a golden crust. Poke a few holes in the tops with a fork to allow steam to escape.* *Bake until the crusts are tall and deeply golden, about 15 minutes.*

STEP	1	2	3
TYPE OF POT PIE	START PIE FILLING	ADD MAIN INGREDIENT, LIQUID + SEASONING	POUR INTO BOWL + BAKE

spicy chili pot pie	*Preheat oven to 400°F. To a large pot over medium-high heat, add:*
	▸ *3 T. **extra-virgin olive oil***
	▸ *2 **onions**, chopped*
	▸ *3 **shallots**, chopped*
	▸ *4 cloves **garlic**, chopped*
	▸ *½ t. **salt***
	Sauté, stirring frequently, for about 3 minutes.
		Stir in:
		▸ *2 (15-oz.) cans **kidney beans**, drained*
		▸ *1 (15-oz.) can **black beans**, drained*
		▸ *1 (28-oz.) can **crushed tomatoes***
		▸ *1 ½ T. **chili powder***
		▸ *¼ to ½ t. **cayenne pepper***
		Simmer for 5 to 10 minutes, then season with a generous dose of more salt to taste.
			Pour the filling into small ovenproof bowls, each three quarters full.
			   *Cut a piece of **puff pastry dough** to fit each bowl, with some overlap. Place the dough on the bowls and fold over the edges. Brush the dough lightly with **egg white** for a golden crust. Poke a few holes in the tops with a fork to allow steam to escape.*
			   Bake until the crusts are tall and deeply golden, about 15 minutes.
			   This makes a lot of filling, so save leftovers for lunch, or freeze for later.

spring vegetable pot pie	*Preheat oven to 400°F. To a large pot over medium-high heat, add:*
	▸ *3 T. **extra-virgin olive oil***
	▸ *2 **spring onions**, chopped*
	▸ *3 **shallots**, chopped*
	▸ *4 cloves **garlic**, chopped*
	▸ *½ t. **salt***
	▸ *Grated zest of 1 **lemon***
	Sauté, stirring frequently, for about 3 minutes.
		Stir in:
		▸ *1 bunch thin **asparagus**, cut into ½-inch segments*
		Cook for 1 minute.
		   In a small bowl, combine:
		▸ *2 c. **vegetable stock**, water, or milk*
		▸ *2 T. **cornstarch***
		Pour into asparagus mixture. Bring to a boil, stirring constantly, and cook until the filling starts to thicken.
		   Remove from the heat and season with more salt to taste.
			Pour the filling into small ovenproof bowls, each three quarters full.
			   *Add a sprinkling of chopped fresh **chives** and crumbled **goat cheese**.*
			   *Cut a piece of **puff pastry dough** to fit each bowl, with some overlap. Place the dough on the bowls and fold over the edges. Brush the dough lightly with **egg white** for a golden crust. Poke a few holes in the tops with a fork to allow steam to escape.*
			   Bake until the crusts are tall and deeply golden, about 15 minutes.

summer pot pie with tomato + goat cheese	*Preheat oven to 400° F. To a large pot over medium-high heat, add:*
	▸ *3 T. **extra-virgin olive oil***
	▸ *2 **onions**, chopped*
	▸ *3 **shallots**, chopped*
	▸ *4 cloves **garlic**, chopped*
	▸ *1 c. diced **zucchini** (¼-inch dice)*
	▸ *½ t. **salt***
	Sauté, stirring frequently, for about 3 minutes.
		Stir in:
		▸ *2 c. **corn** kernels*
		▸ *1 (28-oz.) can **crushed tomatoes***
		Simmer for 5 minutes. Remove from the heat and season with more salt to taste.
			Pour the filling into small ovenproof bowls, each three quarters full.
			   *Sprinkle a few small pieces of **goat cheese** on top of the filling.*
			   *Cut a piece of **puff pastry dough** to fit each bowl, with some overlap. Place the dough on the bowls and fold over the edges. Brush the dough lightly with **egg white** for a golden crust. Poke a few holes in the tops with a fork to allow the steam to escape.*
			   Bake until the crusts are tall and deeply golden, about 15 minutes.

rice bowls serves 4 to 6

I don't own a rice cooker. We had one growing up and it worked wonderfully, but most of the rice that came out of it was straight and white and used as a side dish to a stir-fry. The rice dishes that eventually became of interest to me were the risottos, paellas, and biryanis of the world — none of which are traditionally made in a rice cooker. Instead they are carefully created right on the stovetop (under a watchful eye), using flavorful ingredients and spices from around the world.

The following rice bowls are meant to be one-dish meals. I've included a variety of regional inspirations and flavors, and have made an effort to nutritionally balance out the grains in each bowl by adding greens, vegetables, tofu, nuts, and other healthful, filling ingredients.

WASH OR NOT There are differing opinions on whether or not to rinse rice before cooking. I started rinsing my rice a few years ago and never looked back, as my rice seemed noticeably lighter and fluffier. Washing rice before cooking rinses away starch. Unless I'm making a risotto, I rinse and drain my rice about three times in the same pot I'm going to cook in. Just fill the pot with cold water, swish the grains around, and pour the water out. Repeat until the water isn't cloudy. This will also help keep the grains separated so they won't clump together. For the following rice bowl recipes, you're going to want to rinse. If you end up with clumpy rice, it will be hard to integrate the additional ingredients.

MY FAVORITE KINDS OF RICE

Basmati: Nutty flavor and a low starch content make this rice a great fit for pilafs and other dishes where the grains need to remain separate. Traditionally used in Indian cooking, basmati rice can be drier, lighter, and fluffier than its counterparts.

Jasmine: One of my favorite types of rice, jasmine is a wonderfully fragrant long-grained rice typically used in Thai and Vietnamese cooking. With more starch than, say, basmati, jasmine rice will cling together a bit more, making it easier to eat with chopsticks.

Wild rice: Not technically a rice, but close enough to fit into this section. Wild rice is beautiful, nutty, and has a nice bite to it. It goes well with smoky foods and fruits. Look for wild rice with extra-long grains; it's often the highest quality and a fun change from traditional-length rice grains. Some wild rice grains are over an inch long.

tips
- *There are many types of rice now available in markets. Try a new kind once a month as a good way to expand your cooking palette.*
- *Be sure to cook your rice in a saucepan with a nice thick bottom; thin-bottomed pans will cause the rice at the bottom to scorch and burn.*

STEP	1	2	3
TYPE OF RICE BOWL	**START FLAVOR BASE**	**ADD RICE + LIQUIDS, THEN SIMMER**	**ADD FINISHING TOUCHES**
green curry rice bowl with tofu	In a large saucepan over medium-high heat, sauté: ▸ 2 T. **peanut oil** ▸ 3 cloves **garlic**, chopped ▸ 1 ½ t. **Thai green curry paste** ▸ 1 t. **salt** Cook for about 1 minute.	Stir in: ▸ 2 c. **jasmine rice**, rinsed and drained ▸ 2 (14-oz.) cans **coconut milk** (light is okay) Bring just to a boil, uncovered. Reduce the heat, cover, and simmer for about 10 minutes, or until the rice really starts absorbing the coconut milk. Turn the heat down even lower and let the rice cook until tender, 15 to 20 more minutes. If it starts to get too dry, add more coconut milk or water, 1 T. at a time.	Add: ▸ ½ c. **peanuts** ▸ 1 ½ c. **snow peas** ▸ 4 **green onions**, chopped Fluff with a fork and cover for 5 minutes. Top with grilled extra-firm **tofu** and slivered fresh **basil**.
lemon + basil rice bowl with tofu	In a large saucepan over medium-high heat, sauté: ▸ 2 T. **peanut oil** ▸ 2 cloves **garlic**, minced ▸ 1 t. **salt** Cook for about 1 minute.	Stir in: ▸ 2 c. **basmati rice**, rinsed and drained ▸ 2 ½ c. **water** Bring just to a boil, uncovered. Reduce the heat, cover, and simmer for about 10 minutes, or until the rice really starts absorbing the water. Turn the heat down even lower and let the rice cook until tender, 20 to 25 more minutes. If it starts to get too dry, add more water, 1 T. at a time. Add 10 handfuls of rinsed **greens** or baby spinach, cover again, and let steam for 5 minutes, or until the greens are wilted.	Add: ▸ 1 c. toasted **pine nuts** (see page 16) ▸ Grated zest and juice of 1 **lemon** ▸ ¼ c. slivered **basil** Fluff with a fork. Top with grilled extra-firm **tofu**. Drizzle more lemon juice on top and season with more salt to taste.
red chile rice bowl with lime	In a large saucepan over medium-high heat, sauté: ▸ 2 T. **peanut oil** ▸ 4 to 6 **red chiles**, minced ▸ 1 ½ t. **Thai red curry paste** ▸ 1 t. **salt** ▸ 1 (1-inch) piece **ginger**, grated Cook for about 1 minute.	Stir in: ▸ 2 c. **jasmine rice**, rinsed and drained ▸ 2 (14-oz.) cans **coconut milk** (light is okay) Bring just to a boil, uncovered. Reduce the heat, cover, and simmer for about 10 minutes, or until the rice really starts absorbing the coconut milk. Turn the heat down even lower and let the rice cook until tender, 15 to 20 more minutes. If it starts to get too dry, add more coconut milk or water, 1 T. at a time.	Add: ▸ Juice of 1 **lime** ▸ 1 c. **cashews** Fluff with a fork and top with precooked 1-inch pieces **green beans** and slivered fresh **basil**. Season with more salt to taste.

STEP	1	2	3
TYPE OF RICE BOWL	START FLAVOR BASE	ADD RICE + LIQUIDS, THEN SIMMER	ADD FINISHING TOUCHES
spiced mango rice bowl	In a large saucepan over medium-high heat, sauté: ▸ 2 T. **peanut oil** or ghee ▸ 1 t. ground **cinnamon** ▸ ¼ t. freshly grated **nutmeg** ▸ ½ t. **salt** Cook for about 1 minute.	Stir in: ▸ 2 c. **basmati rice**, rinsed and drained ▸ 2 ½ c. **coconut milk** (light is okay) ▸ 1 c. pureed **mango** ▸ ⅓ c. **brown sugar** ▸ ½ c. **dried cranberries** or currants Bring just to a boil, uncovered. Reduce the heat, cover, and simmer for about 10 minutes, or until the rice really starts absorbing the coconut milk. Turn the heat down even lower and let the rice cook until tender, 20 to 25 more minutes. If it starts to get too dry, add more coconut milk or water, 1 T. at a time.	Fluff with a fork. Serve sprinkled with a bit of brown sugar and chopped mango.
toasted sesame rice bowl	In a large saucepan over medium-high heat, sauté: ▸ 1 T. dark **sesame oil** ▸ 1 T. **peanut oil** ▸ ¼ c. **soy sauce** ▸ 2 cloves **garlic**, minced Cook for about 1 minute.	Stir in: ▸ 2 c. long-grain **brown rice**, washed and drained ▸ 4 c. **water** Bring just to a boil, uncovered. Reduce the heat, cover, and simmer for about 10 minutes, or until the rice really starts absorbing the water. Turn the heat down even lower and let the rice cook until tender, 40 to 45 more minutes. If it starts to get too dry, add more water, 1 T. at a time.	Add: ▸ ½ c. toasted **sesame seeds** (toast as you would the nuts on page 16) ▸ 6 **green onions**, chopped ▸ Half a small bunch of grilled **asparagus**, cut into 1-inch pieces Fluff with a fork. Season with **salt** to taste. Serve with sliced grilled **tofu**.

wild rice bowl with dried cranberries	Fill a large pot with generously salted water.	Stir in:
		▸ 2 c. **wild rice**, washed and drained
		Boil, uncovered, for 55 minutes or so. You will know the rice is done when many of the grains are cracked open and tender, revealing the lighter inside.
		    Remove from the heat and drain off the water.
			Add:
			▸ ½ c. toasted **pine nuts** (see page 16)
			▸ 1 c. slivered **red onions**
			▸ ½ c. dried **cranberries**
			Garnish with more slivered red onions and crumbled **fake bacon**; both look beautiful next to the natural shades of the wild rice.
			    This dish is great served hot or cold.

fondues

I received a beautiful white Le Creuset fondue set for Christmas two years ago and have been making good use of it ever since. I started out conservatively, making classic Swiss fondues on the savory side and chocolate fondues for dessert. I eventually spread my wings a bit, realizing there were many ingredients I could heat up in the pot, and scores of delicious things to dip.

For many the word fondue still conjures up images of burnt-orange and mustard-yellow fondue pots collecting dust in the back of a cupboard – relics of a slightly funkier, bygone era. But fondue has experienced quite a revival in the past few years, and rightfully so. It's the ultimate social, communal meal: fun, easy to prepare, and nothing short of completely indulgent.

You'll need some special equipment for these recipes. There are two primary kinds of fondue, and they use different types of fondue pots. One is for cheese, chocolate, and the like: These fondue pots are typically earthenware, ceramic, or cast iron. You'll want a good, thick base to diffuse heat and prevent scorching. The second type of pot is usually metal and used for frying foods: The metal is good for keeping the oil very hot. All of the recipes in this section use the first type of pot. Pots come with burners that are usually fueled by alcohol, fuel paste, a candle, or electricity.

DIFFERENT THINGS TO DIP

Fruits: sliced bananas, apples, pears, peaches, or pineapples, or dried fruit, orange sections, strawberries, cherries, raspberries, blackberries, or grapes.

Breads: crusty French or Italian bread, pita wedges, fresh tortillas, tortilla chips, croissants, breadsticks, naan, mixed-grain breads, focaccia, or baked polenta cubes.

Blanched vegetables: broccoli, asparagus, green beans, snow peas, or snap peas. Blanch in a pot of lightly salted boiling water for a minute or two to soften them up just a bit. Drain them well before putting them out on a serving tray.

Raw or roasted vegetables: cherry tomatoes, red bell pepper slices, celery sticks, roasted potato wedges, roasted sweet potatoes, or roasted mushrooms.

Cakes and sweet things: angel food cake, graham crackers, marshmallows, tiny brownies, tiny cookies, ladyfingers, shortbread, amaretti, biscotti, crystallized ginger chunks, or meringues.

tips

- *Invest in a good versatile pot that will last a long time. I love my enamel-lined, cast-iron fondue pot. Make sure it's thick-bottomed so nothing scorches.*

- *If you are having a fondue party, have friends bring their pots from home. This way you can have more than a single type of fondue going at once.*

- *Keep your dipping ingredients bite-sized – no bigger than a 1-inch square.*

- *Color-coded dipping forks are a good way to keep track of which fork is whose.*

STEP	1	2	3
TYPE OF FONDUE	PREP INGREDIENTS	COMBINE INGREDIENTS	TRANSFER TO FONDUE POT
classic cheese fondue	Set aside: ▸ 1 clove **garlic**, peeled ▸ 1 lb. **Gruyère cheese**, shredded; or ½ lb. Gruyère + ½ lb. Emmental cheese Toss the cheese with 3 T. **unbleached all-purpose flour**.	Rub the interior of a medium saucepan with the peeled garlic. Place over medium heat and add 1 ¾ c. **dry white wine**. Bring to a simmer and add the cheese mixture, one handful at a time. Stir in ¼ t. freshly grated **nutmeg**. Stir over low heat until smooth and cheese is melted and bubbling. Add a splash or two of **kirsch** (optional). Continue stirring until it starts to bubble just a bit.	Transfer the cheese mixture to a fondue pot and use chunks of Italian or French **bread** for dipping. Continue to stir frequently.
brie + wild mushroom fondue	Set aside: ▸ ½ lb. or more **shiitake, morel,** or **porcini mushrooms,** finely chopped ▸ 1 clove **garlic** clove, minced, or more to taste ▸ 1 lb. cold **brie**, rind trimmed off, cut into small chunks Toss the cheese with 3 T. **unbleached all-purpose flour**.	In a medium saucepan over a medium-high heat, sauté 1 T. **olive oil** and the mushrooms and garlic. Sauté for 4 minutes, then add 1 c. **dry white wine**. Bring to a simmer and add the cheese mixture, one handful at a time. Stir over low heat until smooth and cheese is melted and bubbling.	Transfer the cheese and mushroom mixture to a fondue pot and use chunks of Italian, French, or mixed-grain **bread** for dipping. Blanched vegetables like **asparagus** spears or **green beans** are also good. Continue to stir frequently.
chipotle fondue	Set aside: ▸ 2 t. **adobo sauce** from a can of chipotle chiles ▸ 1 lb. **Gruyère cheese**, shredded Toss the cheese with 3 T. **unbleached all-purpose flour**.	Place a medium saucepan over medium heat and add 1 ¾ c. **dry white wine**. Bring to a simmer and add the cheese mixture, one handful at a time. Stir over low heat until smooth and the cheese is melted and bubbling. Add the adobo sauce; if you like it really spicy and smoky, add more to taste. Continue stirring until it starts to bubble again.	Transfer the chipotle mixture to a fondue pot and use grilled **tofu** squares, fresh **tortilla wedges, baguette** cubes, **red bell pepper** strips, or **tortilla chips** for dipping. Continue to stir frequently.

STEP	1	2	3
TYPE OF FONDUE	PREP INGREDIENTS	COMBINE INGREDIENTS	TRANSFER TO FONDUE POT
goat cheese fondue	Set aside: ▸ 1 clove **garlic**, peeled ▸ 1 lb. soft **goat cheese**, crumbled Toss the crumbled cheese with 3 T. **unbleached all-purpose flour**.	Rub the interior of a medium saucepan with the peeled garlic. Place over medium heat and add 1 ½ c. **heavy cream**. Bring to a simmer and add the cheese mixture, one handful at a time Stir over low heat until smooth and the cheese is melted and bubbling.	Transfer the cheese mixture to a fondue pot and use sliced **apples**, **pears**, and a variety of **breads** for dipping. Continue to stir frequently.
spicy bean fondue	Set aside: ▸ 2 (15-oz.) cans mild **vegetarian chili** (or equivalent amount of homemade chili)	To a medium saucepan over medium heat, add the chili. When the chili is hot, stir in: ▸ 1 c. **light cream cheese** ▸ ¾ t. **cayenne pepper** Stir until nice and creamy. The cheese should be melted and well integrated.	Transfer the chili and cheese mixture to a fondue pot and use grilled **tofu** squares, fresh **tortilla wedges**, or **tortilla chips** for dipping. Continue to stir frequently.
SWEET FONDUE **chocolate fondue**	Set aside: ▸ 1 lb. premium semisweet or **bittersweet chocolate**, well chopped	In a medium saucepan over low heat, place: ▸ 1½ c. **heavy cream** Bring to a simmer and add the chocolate. Simmer, stirring, until the chocolate is melted.	Transfer the chocolate mixture to a fondue pot and use **strawberries**, **cherries**, **orange** sections, **graham crackers**, **marshmallows**, or **ladyfingers** for dipping. Continue to stir frequently.
SWEET FONDUE **marsh-mallow fondue**	Set aside: ▸ 1 lb. **marshmallows** (see Resources on page 186 for information on purchasing vegan marshmallows).	In a medium saucepan over low heat, combine: ▸ 1½ c. **heavy cream** ▸ 2 T. **unbleached all-purpose flour** Bring to a simmer and add the marshmallows. Stir until the marshmallows are melted. Whisk in a splash of your favorite flavored liqueur for a boost of flavor; I like **amaretto** or apricot brandy.	Transfer the chocolate mixture to a fondue pot and use **fruits**, cubes of **Roasted Winter Squash** (page 111), **meringues**, or thin **chocolate wafers** for dipping. Continue to stir frequently.

stir-fries

Stir-frying is hot, fast, furious, and exciting. It's the fifty-yard dash of the culinary world. One minute you've got hissing, crackling, and splattering, the next minute everything is quiet, calm, and you have a delicious plate of food in front of you. If things aren't getting a little crazy when you're stir-frying, you probably aren't doing it quite right. The idea is to cook bite-sized bits of food over intense heat, all the while stirring and tossing to prevent sticking and burning.

Keep these things in mind when making stir-fries: You need to keep the heat high; the cooking times are quick; and there is usually quite a long list of ingredients you need to prepare ahead of time. These recipes do not feed more than 2 people, because you'll end up with steam-fried food if you add too much to the pan at once. (The temperature in the pan will drop way down if you try to fill it up.) Cook in batches if you have a crowd on your hands.

All that being said, don't be intimidated! Stir-fries might be a bit tricky at first, but they become easy and fun after a bit of practice. It's the kind of dish where you need to jump in with both feet. Read a few of the following tips, and start chopping.

tips

- *Make sure you read through the recipe and have a game plan before starting; you may not have much time to refer back to the book once you fire up the wok.*
- *Get absolutely everything prepped, chopped, and ready to go before you actually start stir-frying or you'll still be chopping while the rest of your ingredients are burning.*

- *If you don't have a wok, use a large skillet, one that can handle the highest heat your stove burner can put out. The thin walls of a wok conduct heat quickly and in turn zap anything directly touching the wok or pan very quickly. This is the reason you need to keep stirring constantly.*
- *Use oils that are able to stand up to the high temperatures of stir-frying without burning. Peanut and canola are both good choices. Butter, on the other hand, is not a good choice as it has a much lower smoking point.*

- *Many Chinese restaurants have open kitchens. Next time you're in one, keep an eye on the stir-fry chefs. Observe their timing, how they toss the food around, and the way they use utensils. This may be a stretch for the home kitchen, but you'll certainly pick up some techniques from watching.*

CITRUS TOFU, LONG BEAN + WALNUT STIR-FRY

STEP	1	2	3
TYPE OF STIR-FRY	PREP INGREDIENTS	STIR-FRY	ADD FINISHING TOUCHES
citrus tofu, long bean + walnut stir-fry	Set next to the stove: ▸ 1 (8-oz.) package extra-firm **tofu**, cut into slices 1 inch long and about as thick as a pencil ▸ 1 **shallot**, thinly sliced ▸ 2 small **red chiles**, chopped ▸ 1 ½ c. **long beans** or green beans, cut on the bias into 1-inch segments ▸ 2 T. **hoisin sauce**, diluted in 1/4 c. water ▸ Grated zest and juice of 1 **orange** ▸ 1 handful **walnut** pieces ▸ 1 generous handful fresh **basil**, slivered (optional)	Place a wok or large nonstick pan over high heat and add a splash of **peanut oil**. When the oil is very hot, add the tofu. Cook for 3 to 4 minutes, until golden brown. Stir every couple minutes to brown all over. Remove the tofu from the pan and set aside. Return the pan to the heat and add another splash of oil. As soon as it's hot, add the shallot, chiles, and beans. Stir for 1 to 2 minutes. Add the hoisin mixture, and cook for another minute, until the beans are just tender. Add the orange zest and juice and return the tofu to the pan. Cook for 1 more minute, stirring.	Turn off the heat and stir in the walnuts and basil, if using. Add a quick dash of **salt**. Serve immediately, preferably with steamed **jasmine rice**.
heidi's favorite stir-fry	Set next to the stove: ▸ 1 (8-oz.) package extra-firm **tofu**, cut into slices 1 inch long and about as thick as a pencil ▸ 3 cloves **garlic**, minced ▸ 5 **green onions**, chopped ▸ 1 (1-inch) piece **ginger**, peeled and grated ▸ 3 small **red chiles**, chopped ▸ 1 ½ c. chopped thin **asparagus** (1-inch pieces cut on the bias) ▸ 1 handful **cashews**, chopped or crushed ▸ Grated zest and juice of 1 **lime** ▸ 2 T. **hoisin sauce** ▸ 1 small handful fresh **mint**, slivered ▸ 1 small handful of fresh **basil**, slivered	Place a wok or large nonstick pan over high heat and add a splash of **peanut oil**. When the oil is very hot, add the tofu. Cook for 3 to 4 minutes, until golden brown. Stir every couple minutes to brown all over. Remove the tofu from the pan and set aside. Return the pan to the heat and add another splash of oil. As soon as it's hot, add the garlic, green onions, ginger, chiles, and asparagus. Stir for 1 to 2 minutes. Add the cashews and keep stirring for another minute. Return the tofu to the pan. Stir in the lime zest and juice, as well as the hoisin sauce. Cook for 1 to 2 more minutes, stirring.	Turn off the heat and stir in the mint and basil, with a dash of **salt**. Serve immediately, preferably with steamed **jasmine rice**.

STEP	1	2	3
TYPE OF STIR-FRY	PREP INGREDIENTS	STIR-FRY	ADD FINISHING TOUCHES

mixed green stir-fry	Set next to the stove:
	▸ 4 cloves **garlic**, chopped
	▸ ½ t. **red-pepper flakes**
	▸ 16 to 20 big handfuls of **mixed greens**, well washed and cut into 1-inch-wide ribbons (any combination of spinach, bok choy, mustard greens, etc., will work)
	▸ 1 T. toasted **sesame seeds** (see page 16)
		Place a large wok or extra-large nonstick pan over high heat and add a splash of **peanut oil**. When the oil is very hot, add the garlic and red-pepper flakes. Stir for 30 seconds.
		   Add all the greens and stir for another minute, until tender and wilted.
			Turn off the heat and stir in 5 pinches of **salt**.
			   Drizzle with 2 t. dark **sesame oil**. Serve immediately, sprinkled with sesame seeds.

noodles stir-fried with asian greens	Set next to the stove:
	▸ 3 cloves **garlic**, minced
	▸ 2 small **red chiles**, chopped
	▸ 10 handfuls **Asian greens**, well washed and dried
	▸ 2 T. **hoisin sauce**
	▸ 1 T. **soy sauce**
	Cook ½ lb. fresh **Asian egg noodles** in a pot of boiling water until tender. Drain, rinse, and set aside. You can find these noodles in the refrigerator section of your market.
		Place a wok or large nonstick pan over high heat and add a splash of **peanut oil**. When the oil is very hot, add the garlic and chiles. Stir for 30 seconds.
		   Add as much of the greens as the pan will hold and stir for another minute, until tender and wilted. Add the remaining greens as the cooked ones shrink down.
		   Stir in the hoisin and soy sauces, then add the noodles. Stir well and remove from the heat.
			Season with a sprinkling of chopped **green onions**.

spicy green bean + mushroom stir-fry	Set next to the stove:
	▸ 2 cloves **garlic**, chopped
	▸ ¼ t. **red-pepper flakes**
	▸ ½ lb. **mushrooms**, sliced
	▸ 1 ½ c. chopped **long beans** or **green beans** (1-inch pieces cut on the bias)
	▸ ½ t. **chile oil**
	▸ 1 T. **soy sauce**
	▸ ¼ c. crushed **peanuts**
		Place a wok or large nonstick pan over high heat and add a splash of **peanut oil** or roasted peanut oil. When the oil is very hot, add the garlic and red-pepper flakes. Stir for 1 minute, or until the garlic is golden. Add the mushrooms and stir for 30 seconds or so, until the mushrooms release their liquid.
		   Add the beans and stir for 2 to 3 minutes, until the beans are cooked through but still have a bit of a bite.
		   Stir in the chile oil and soy sauce.
			Turn off the heat and stir in **salt** to taste (don't skimp here). Serve immediately, sprinkled with the peanuts.

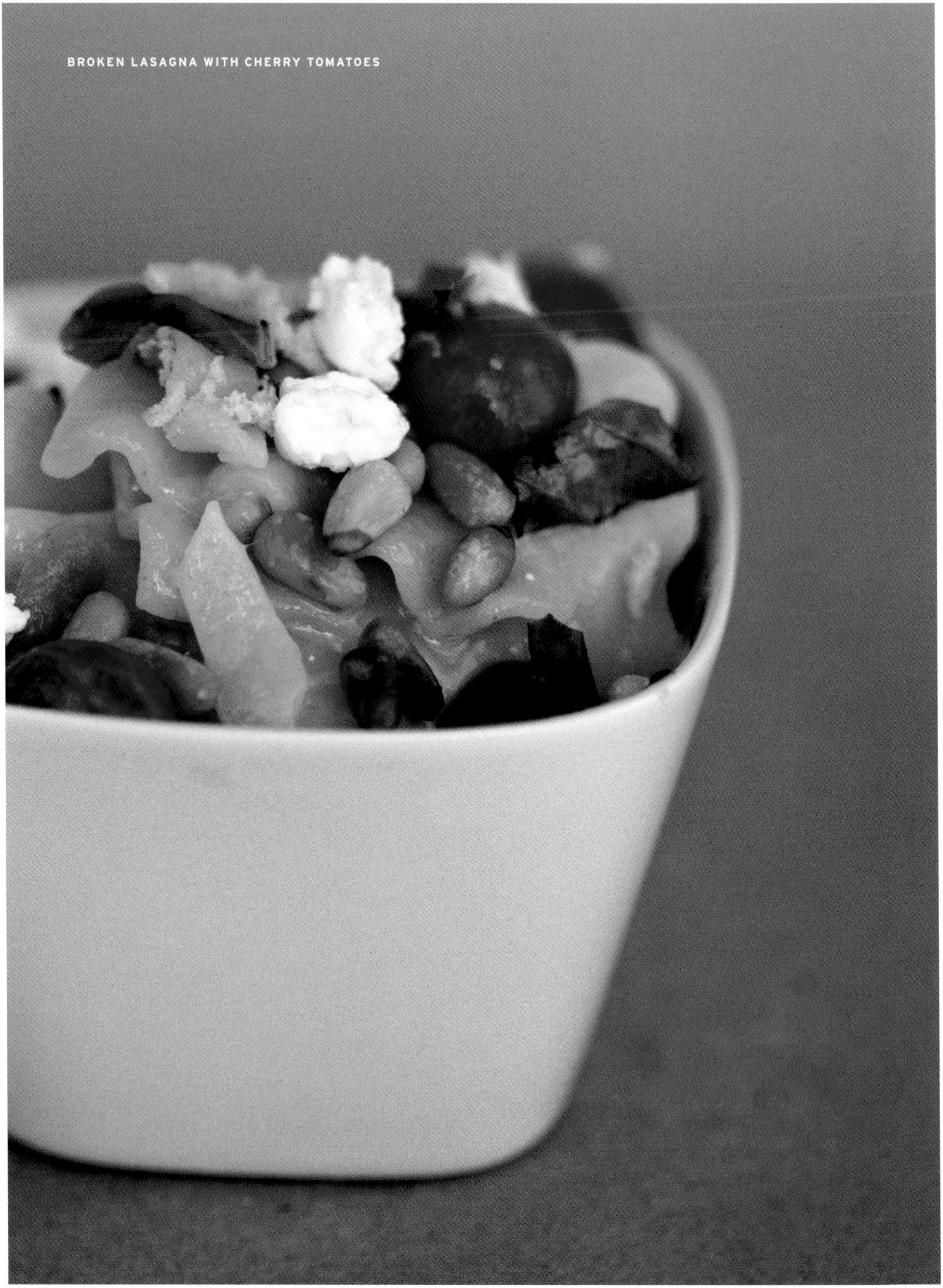

BROKEN LASAGNA WITH CHERRY TOMATOES

pasta dishes SERVES 4 TO 6

Pasta dishes are perfect for the time-challenged. Boiling the water often takes longer than getting everything else ready.

In preparation for the inevitable night when I need to whip something up using whatever I have in the house, I try to keep some personal favorites on hand. I always, always keep a few different kinds of pasta in the cupboard and a chunk of Parmesan in the refrigerator, next to the pine nuts and walnuts. Olives and sun-dried tomatoes are in the pantry, and, if I'm lucky and my basil plants haven't shriveled up, I'll have some fresh herbs as well. Plenty of ingredients to play with.

I've included a variety of different pasta dishes here. Some are packed with healthful greens and vegetables; others are a bit more indulgent, and use a heavier hand with the cream and cheese. All are very tasty and quick to prepare.

A FEW TYPES OF PASTA

Small: Small pasta can be very cute. With names like butterflies (farfalle) and little ears (orecchiette), it's a fun way to add whimsy and imagination to your pasta dishes. Many of them have shapes, folds, and pockets that are great for holding a range of sauces, from creamy to chunky. The tiniest of pastas, like orzo and stelline (little stars), are best for salads, soups, and stews.

Thin: Spaghetti, angel hair, and linguine are a few of the better known and more commonly used noodles. I like to keep sauces for this type of pasta simple: A splash of good olive oil, a simple red sauce, or a light cream sauce are all good choices. I also try to remember not to toss a bunch of chunky stuff like olives or nuts into the pan because they always end up at the bottom, instead of mixed in with the noodles. Wait until serving, and then sprinkle the chunky bits on top.

Wide: A general rule of thumb to keep in mind here: Big noodles need big sauce and big flavor. Wide pastas include fettuccini, lasagna, and pappardelle. You want a sauce – like an alfredo or a chunky red sauce – that can offer up a nice flavorful coating all across the pasta.

Tube: Tubular pasta comes in a range of sizes. It can be very tiny, large enough to stuff, and anything in between. It also tends to have either ridges or no ridges. I like to use tube-shaped pasta for all sorts of baked pasta dishes and casseroles. It also goes well with hearty chunky red sauces and cheese that clings to any ridges and gets inside it. Penne, rigatoni, macaroni, and ziti are all examples.

tips

- *If you are serious about making a great bowl of pasta, you need to start by getting out a big pot and filling it with plenty of water. Just before adding the pasta, add a good dose of salt to the rapidly boiling water. The Italians like to get their pasta water as salty as the Mediterranean. I use a small palmful of sea salt, roughly 3 T.*

- *I could write a whole page on fresh pasta versus dried pasta, but I'll condense it down to this: Making fresh pasta is a great project for a slow Saturday, since it's a bit of a time commitment. It's wonderful in many baked pasta dishes. Dried pasta, on the other hand, is very convenient, not perishable, and has nice texture and bite for pasta dishes like the ones that follow.*

- *Don't throw out your leftover pasta. Put any leftovers you have in an appropriately sized casserole dish. When you're ready to reheat, sprinkle the casserole with bread crumbs and shredded Parmesan and bake at 350°F until the top is golden and the pasta is heated through.*

STEP	1	2	3
TYPE OF PASTA DISH	PREP INGREDIENTS	BOIL PASTA	ADD FINISHING TOUCHES
broken lasagna with cherry tomatoes	Prep and set aside: ► 1 lb. **lasagna noodles**, broken into 1-inch pieces ► 15 to 20 tiny **cherry tomatoes**, halved ► 1 c. freshly grated **Parmesan cheese** ► 1 c. toasted **pine nuts** (see page 16) ► 1 c. toasted **bread crumbs** ► 2 handfuls fresh **basil**, slivered	Boil the pasta pieces in a large pot of salted water according to the package instructions or until just tender. Drain and immediately return the pasta to the pot over medium heat.	Gently stir in 2 T. **extra-virgin olive oil** (or more to taste), the cherry tomatoes, cheese, and pine nuts. Season with **s+p** to taste. Stir in the bread crumbs and basil. Serve immediately, topped with crumbled **goat cheese**.
favorite fettuccini alfredo	Prep and set aside: ► 1 ½ c. **heavy cream** ► 3 T. **unsalted butter** ► 1 c. freshly grated **Parmesan cheese**.	Boil 1 lb. fresh **fettuccini** in a large pot of salted water according to the package instructions or until just tender. While the pasta is boiling, heat the cream in a small saucepan. Drain the pasta and immediately return it to the pot over medium heat.	Stir in the cream and butter. Add the cheese and **s+p** to taste. I also love to add a couple cups of sautéed sliced mushrooms to this. Chopped fake bacon on top is also a plus.
pasta with bright red tomato sauce	Prep and set aside: ► 3 ½ c. **Bright Red Tomato Sauce** (page 126) ► 2 handfuls **kalamata olives**, pitted and torn into pieces ► 1 c. fresh **basil**, slivered	Boil 1 lb. fresh or dried **linguine** in a large pot of salted water according to the package instructions or until just tender. Drain and immediately return the pasta to the pot over medium heat.	Stir in the Bright Red Tomato Sauce. Add the olives and basil. Serve immediately, topped with plenty of freshly grated **Parmesan cheese**.

STEP	1	2	3
TYPE OF PASTA DISH	PREP INGREDIENTS	BOIL PASTA	ADD FINISHING TOUCHES
saffron corkscrews with peas + parmesan	Prep and set aside: ▸ 1 ½ c. fresh or frozen **peas** ▸ 1 ½ c. **heavy cream** ▸ A small pinch of **saffron** threads (about 15 threads) ▸ 1 cup freshly grated **Parmesan cheese** ▸ 1 generous handful toasted **pine nuts** (see page 16)	Boil 1 lb. **corkscrew pasta** (fusilli) in a large pot of salted water according to the package instructions or until you have about 1 minute left to boil; add the peas. While the pasta is boiling, heat the heavy cream in a small saucepan with the saffron. Drain and immediately return the pasta and peas to the pot over medium heat.	Stir in the saffron cream mixture, the Parmesan cheese, and **salt** to taste. Sprinkle the pine nuts on top of each serving bowl. This is also great sprinkled with chopped fake bacon.
spring butterflies with lemon cream	Prep and set aside: ▸ 1 large bunch pencil-thin **asparagus**, cut on the bias into 1-inch pieces ▸ 1 ½ c. **heavy cream** ▸ ½ c. **milk** ▸ 1 c. freshly grated **Parmesan cheese** ▸ Grated zest of 3 **lemons** ▸ 1 handful fresh **basil**, slivered	Boil 1 lb. dried **butterfly pasta** (farfalle) in a large pot of salted water according to the package instructions or until you have about 1 minute left to boil; add the asparagus. Drain and immediately return the pasta and asparagus to the pot over medium heat. While the pasta is boiling, heat the cream and milk in a small saucepan.	Stir the cream mixture into the pasta and add the cheese and lemon zest. Sprinkle with the basil. Season with **salt** to taste. Top with any of the following: **Crystallized lemon zest**, crushed **pine nuts**, **red-pepper flakes**, more Parmesan.
whole wheat penne with wilted spinach	Prep and set aside: ▸ 3 T. **unsalted butter**, cut into small chunks ▸ 8 handfuls fresh **spinach**, washed and cut into 1-inch ribbons ▸ ½ c. plump dried **apricots**, chopped ▸ ½ c. toasted **pine nuts** (see page 16) ▸ 1 c. shredded **Parmesan cheese** ▸ ¾ c. crumbled **feta cheese**	Boil 1 lb. **whole wheat penne** in a large pot of salted water according to the package instructions or until just tender. Drain and immediately return the pasta to the pot over medium heat.	Stir in the butter, spinach, and apricots. Cook over medium-high heat for 2 to 3 minutes, until the spinach is wilted and tender. Stir in the pine nuts, Parmesan, and a couple pinches of **salt**. Gently stir in the feta and serve immediately.

risottos MAKES A FAMILY-SIZED POT OF RISOTTO

Risotto has a well-earned reputation for being tricky and difficult to perfect. There are a lot of rules for making risotto, many of which, it seems, are okay to ignore as long as you get the basics right. Risotto is similar in scope to a pilaf or paella in that the ingredients are added and absorbed into the rice, imparting various flavors to the dish. There is much discussion regarding different types of rice, the proper stock, when to add liquid, what type of pot to use – all factors that, when properly aligned, can turn your dish into a rich, creamy risotto with a base of plump yet structured grains.

I have run into most, if not all, of the pitfalls of risotto making: scorched rice, undercooked grains, oversalted, undersalted, generally flavorless, and soupy – just to name a few. These have all proven helpful as I stumbled my way toward a perfect pot. This risotto should come out on the thick and creamy side. What you are shooting for is a too-thick-to-pour, but not-thick-enough-to-scoop consistency.

THE RICE My rice of choice for risotto is Arborio, but Carnaroli works equally well. I just grab whichever I have on hand. They're both medium-grain Italian rices and usually say "superfino" on the box or bag. The grains are plump and a little rounded. Don't try to swap in other types of rice if you are going for an authentic risotto – this is one of those cases where it pays to stick with tradition.

THE LIQUID I like bright, clean, simple yet rich-tasting risotto. I choose not to use stock, for which I take a bit of heat from stock enthusiasts. Many people say the key to a good risotto is a good stock. I've made risotto with homemade vegetable stock, bouillon cubes, and canned stock (low-sodium and regular). The minute I start adding these, I lose a lot of control over my salt and my flavors.

The following risotto recipes typically have one flavor that I want to really shine through, and keeping it simple helps facilitate this. I compensate by going a bit heavier on the onions and garlic in the beginning, and using a good table wine as part of the base. I also haven't found it necessary to heat the liquids before adding them, although many people do this.

tips

- Unlike with the Rice Bowl recipes (pages 68–71), never rinse your rice when cooking risotto. You need the starch to get that perfect creamy risotto texture.
- You'll want to have everything chopped and ready to go before you start cooking risotto. Once you turn on that stove burner, you only have a few minutes before most of your ingredients need to be in the pot.
- When a recipe calls for a dry white wine, it just means a wine that isn't sweet. Sauvignon Blanc or Chardonnay are both good choices. I've also used vermouth or a dry sherry.
- You should find the right pot. A heavy-bottomed one is important. I love to cook risotto in my cast-iron, enamel-lined Le Creuset French oven pot. It holds a few quarts, and it's thick, heavy, and distributes heat perfectly. If your pan is too wide, the liquid will evaporate too quickly. If it's too narrow, it will do just the opposite.
- If rice is starting to stick to the bottom of your saucepan, or if it's scorching and turning brown (burning), keep stirring and turn down your heat a bit. Also, I always use a wooden spoon for stirring risotto. This way the pot doesn't get damaged and the handle stays nice and cool.
- If you have leftovers, just reheat the risotto on the stove over low heat, stirring in a bit of water to cream it all up again.
- Since you're only using a handful of ingredients, don't skimp on the quality. Use fresh herbs, good-quality cheeses, and wine you would actually drink.

CITRUS RISOTTO

STEP	1	2	3	4
TYPE OF RISOTTO	START SAUTÉING BASE	STIR IN RICE	ADD LIQUIDS	ADD FINISHING TOUCHES
basic risotto	To a thick-bottomed saucepan over medium heat, add: ▸ 3 T. **unsalted butter** ▸ 3 cloves **garlic**, minced ▸ 1 **onion**, minced ▸ A pinch of **salt** Sauté for about 4 minutes, stirring constantly.	Stir 2 c. **Arborio rice** into the saucepan. Stir continuously for about 3 minutes, coating the rice grains with butter. You want the grains to begin to look translucent around the edges.	Stir in: ▸ 1 c. **dry white wine** When the wine is absorbed, add: ▸ 2 c. **water** Add about 3 more cups water, 1 cup at a time, letting the rice absorb the liquid between each addition. Keep stirring. When your risotto is creamy but still has a bite to it (al dente), after about 23 minutes, you're ready for the next step.	Stir in: ▸ 1 T. unsalted butter ▸ ¾ c. freshly grated **Parmesan cheese** ▸ ¼ c. **mascarpone** (optional) Season with a generous amount of salt and freshly ground **pepper**.
citrus risotto	To a thick-bottomed saucepan over medium heat, add: ▸ 3 T. **unsalted butter** ▸ 3 cloves **garlic**, minced ▸ 1 **onion**, minced ▸ A pinch of **salt** Sauté for about 4 minutes, stirring constantly.	Stir 2 c. **Arborio rice** into the saucepan. Stir continuously for about 3 minutes, coating the rice grains with butter. You want the grains to begin to look translucent around the edges.	Stir in: ▸ 1 c. **dry white wine** When the wine is absorbed, add: ▸ 2 c. **water** Add about 3 more cups of water, 1 cup at a time, letting the rice absorb the liquid between each addition. Keep stirring. When your risotto is creamy but still has a bite to it (al dente), after about 23 minutes, you're ready for the next step.	Stir in: ▸ Grated zest and juice of 1 **lemon** ▸ Grated zest, the segments, and juice of 2 small **oranges** (for segments, cut out the pith and membranes with a serrated knife and tear segments up a bit before adding) ▸ ½ c. freshly grated **Parmesan cheese** ▸ ¼ c. **mascarpone** Season with a generous amount of salt.

STEP	1	2	3	4
TYPE OF RISOTTO	START SAUTÉING BASE	STIR IN RICE	ADD LIQUIDS	ADD FINISHING TOUCHES
herb garden risotto	To a thick-bottomed saucepan over medium heat, add: ▸ 3 T. **unsalted butter** ▸ 3 cloves **garlic**, minced ▸ 1 **onion**, minced ▸ A pinch of **salt** Sauté for about 4 minutes, stirring constantly.	Stir 2 c. **Arborio rice** into the saucepan. Stir continuously for about 3 minutes, coating the rice grains with butter. You want the grains to begin to look translucent around the edges.	Stir in: ▸ 1 c. **dry white wine** When the wine is absorbed, add: ▸ 2 c. **water** Add about 3 more cups water, 1 cup at a time, letting the rice absorb the liquid between each addition. Keep stirring. (I sometimes throw in a few handfuls of peas or thin asparagus tips here.) When your risotto is creamy but still has a bite to it (al dente), after about 23 minutes, you're ready for the next step.	Stir in: ▸ ¾ c. freshly grated **Parmesan cheese** ▸ ¼ c. **mascarpone** (optional) Sprinkle with: ▸ 1 c. loosely packed fresh **basil** leaves, finely slivered ▸ 2 bunches fresh **chives**, chopped (about ½ c.) ▸ 1 c. rinsed **spinach** leaves, finely chopped Season with a generous amount of salt. Garnish with toasted **pine nuts** (see page 16).
tomato risotto	To a thick-bottomed saucepan over medium heat, add: ▸ 3 T. **unsalted butter** ▸ 3 cloves **garlic**, minced ▸ 1 **onion**, minced ▸ A pinch of **salt** Sauté for about 4 minutes, stirring constantly.	Stir 2 c. **Arborio rice** into the saucepan. Stir continuously for about 3 minutes, coating the rice grains with butter. You want the grains to begin to look translucent around the edges.	Stir in: ▸ 1 c. **dry white wine** When the wine is absorbed, add 1 (14-oz.) can **diced tomatoes** with liquid. When the liquid is absorbed, add the rest of the can of tomatoes, and about 2 more cups water, 1 cup at a time, letting the rice absorb the liquid between each addition. Keep stirring. When your risotto is creamy but still has a bite to it (al dente), after 25 to 30 minutes, you're ready for the next step.	Stir in: ▸ ¾ c. freshly grated **Parmesan cheese**, or more to taste ▸ ¼ c. **mascarpone**, or more to taste Season with a generous amount of salt and plenty of slivered fresh **basil**.

CHAPTER 4.0

SIDES

green salads / smooth soups / chunky chowders /
mashed potatoes / roasted vegetables

green salads serves 4 to 6

Arugula, endive, butter lettuce, frisée, escarole, radicchio, tatsoi, mâche, and romaine are only a handful of the vast selection of salad greens that are now readily available in produce sections and farmers' markets around the country. With so many exciting types of salad greens out there of various flavor, color, and texture, I encourage you to try new ones and experiment with different toppings and dressings.

I have a few favorite salads that are perfect for spring and summer and others I make during fall and winter. All are included here. One of the great things I've come to appreciate about making a good salad is that there aren't many rules. There are a few basic guidelines, but after that it's all about personal preference. These salads are simple and quick, especially if you prepare your vinaigrette in advance. I always try to include a little something crunchy, a little something sweet, and lots of perfect greens in each salad.

FAVORITE TYPES OF SALAD GREENS

Baby spinach: My everyday favorite. I eat more baby spinach than anyone else I know. It makes a beautiful bright green base that works well in many types of salads. You want to look for tender, small leaves. If the leaves you're finding have too much stem, just take the extra time to snap them off, leaving the leaves intact. It only takes a few minutes and makes a big difference.

Butter lettuce: With soft, curvy leaves that are often pale green in color, butter lettuce is delicious, mild, and beautiful. I love to use it in salads with oranges. Makes a great base for a lunch or summertime salad.

Herbs: If you've never used fresh, whole herbs in your salads, I'm here to tell you it's time to start! They add such a burst of amazing flavor — they make the difference between an average salad and an extraordinary one. I love using chives (and chive flowers), whole basil leaves (and flowers), mint, and cilantro.

tips

- *Washing greens: Be nice to your salad greens. They are easily damaged and bruised by rough handling. To wash them, dunk greens (already trimmed) into a big bowl or sink of the coldest water you can get out of your tap. Gently swirl them around to release any dirt.*

- *Dry your greens very well after you wash them. It's important to get as much water as possible off of your salad greens. I usually give mine a quick twirl in a salad spinner. For good measure, I also toss a few paper towels into the salad bowl to soak up any remaining water, and remove the towels before tossing. Dressing will cling only to dry greens.*

- *Buy the freshest greens you can. Pass on anything that looks wilted, discolored, or generally un-perky. If you somehow end up with*

wilting greens, run them under very cold water for a minute or two.

- *Don't toss your salad with dressing until right before serving. Even better, toss at the table. If you accidentally overdress your salad, just add in a few extra greens and toss again.*

- *As a rule, don't serve green salads on warm plates. You want your plates nice and cool, or at the very least room temperature.*

RED-LEAF SALAD WITH POMEGRANATE VINAIGRETTE

STEP	1	2	3
TYPE OF GREEN SALAD	GET SALAD GREENS READY	CHOP + PREP ANY OTHER ADD-INS	TOSS + SERVE
basic tiny greens with olive oil + salt	*Make this salad only if you can find 6 to 8 handfuls extra fresh baby or tiny greens. Any combination will do: baby spinach, arugula, mâche, etc. Put in a large bowl.*	*This salad needs absolutely nothing besides great greens and a toss of the following simple dressing.*	*Toss ingredients well in a large bowl with:* ‣ *1 T. best-quality extra-virgin olive oil* ‣ *⅛ t. salt* ‣ *A pinch of freshly ground pepper*
baby spinach salad with mediter-ranean goodies	*Put in a large bowl:* ‣ *6 to 8 handfuls baby spinach, washed and well dried*	*Add:* ‣ *A couple handfuls toasted pine nuts (see page 16)* ‣ *1 handful kalamata olives, pitted and torn into small pieces* ‣ *15 to 20 small cherry tomatoes, halved or quartered* ‣ *2 handfuls of Homemade Croutons (see page 16)* ‣ *½ c. slivered fresh basil*	*Toss well, with:* ‣ *About ⅓ c. Basic French Vinaigrette (page 131).* *Sprinkle with:* ‣ *½ c. crumbled feta cheese.*
butter lettuce sunshine salad	*Put in a large bowl:* ‣ *6 to 8 handfuls butter lettuce leaves, torn into bite-sized pieces, washed and well dried (about 2 medium heads)*	*Add:* ‣ *1 or 2 medium oranges, torn into pieces, skin and pith removed* ‣ *1 avocado, thinly sliced* ‣ *½ c. toasted slivered almonds (see page 16)* ‣ *½ small red onion, slivered*	*Toss well, with:* ‣ *About ⅓ c. Citrus-Parmesan Vinaigrette (page 131).* *Sprinkle with:* ‣ *A few shavings Parmesan cheese (you can make nice, thick curls by using a vegetable peeler).*
herb salad with edible flowers	*Put in a large bowl:* ‣ *5 handfuls arugula* ‣ *1 to 2 handfuls of a mix of fresh basil leaves, chives, and mint, washed and well dried*	*Add:* ‣ *1 handful toasted slivered almonds (see page 16)* ‣ *1 handful goat cheese, crumbled*	*Toss well, with:* ‣ *About ⅓ c. Mint-Orange Vinaigrette (page 133)* *Sprinkle with:* ‣ *Edible flowers* *Note: Many produce sections now have a small selection of edible flowers. Rose petals and violets come in a variety of colors and add an unexpected burst of color to a salad.*

STEP	1	2	3
TYPE OF GREEN SALAD	GET SALAD GREENS READY	CHOP + PREP ANY OTHER ADD-INS	TOSS + SERVE
mixed greens with blue cheese + walnuts	Put in a large bowl: ▸ *6 to 8 handfuls **mixed greens**, washed and well dried*	Add: ▸ *2 handfuls toasted **walnut** pieces (see page 16)* ▸ *½ c. crumbled **blue cheese*** ▸ *1 red **apple**, cored and cut into small slices, peel left on* ▸ *2 handfuls **Homemade Croutons** (page 16; optional)*	Toss well, with: ▸ *About ⅓ c. **Cranberry-Mustard Vinaigrette** (page 131)* Note: *Out of all the salads I make, I get the most requests for this one. It's a staple at family gatherings, and a great salad to make during the holidays because of the walnuts and the pretty red apples.*
pretty summer salad	Put in a large bowl: ▸ *6 to 8 handfuls **baby spinach**, mixed greens, or arugula, washed and well dried*	Add: ▸ *10 **cherry tomatoes**, halved or quartered* ▸ *2 handfuls **Homemade Croutons** (page 16)* ▸ *½ c. fresh **basil**, slivered* ▸ *½ small **red onion**, thinly sliced* ▸ *2 c. **green beans**, blanched in boiling water for 1 minute, then dunked into cold water to stop the cooking* ▸ *1 c. fresh **corn** kernels*	Toss well, with: ▸ *About ⅓ c. **Fresh Herb Vinaigrette** (page 132)* Sprinkle with: ▸ *½ c. crumbled **goat cheese***
red-leaf salad with pome-granate vinaigrette	Put in a large bowl: ▸ *6 to 8 handfuls **red-leaf salad greens**, washed and well dried*	Add: ▸ *½ c. **golden raisins*** ▸ *½ c. **dried cranberries*** ▸ *1 **pear** or apple, sliced* ▸ *2 handfuls toasted **pecans** or walnuts (see page 16)*	Toss well, with: ▸ *About ⅓ c. **Pomegranate Vinaigrette** (page 133)*

smooth soups

One of my favorite things to do during the week is to take one of the vintage streetcars down Market Street to the San Francisco Museum of Modern Art and swing by the café. They have a delicious new flavor of soup every day, always vegetarian. I get a bowl of it with a piece of fresh focaccia and a small bowl of mixed olives, and enjoy a nice lunch before going upstairs to look at the current exhibits.

Once I figured out the basic approach to making good, quick soups, it has been easy to adapt the recipe using whatever vegetable or bean I feel like.

I've all but given up on making soup that requires a separate recipe for stock. Not everyone has homemade stock on hand, and often store-bought stock has an astro-nomical amount of sodium in it. In creating these recipes, I made the assumption that many of you are in the same boat as I am: no stock on hand and lack of time and motivation to make one. By using a generous base of onions, shallots, and garlic, these recipes pack a fresh and flavorful punch. If you do have a favorite vegetable stock on hand, great: Use it. Go ahead and swap it in place of the water called for in each of these recipes. If not, don't sweat it. You'll still be able to create delicious soups in a flash and have plenty of leftovers to spare.

The following soups freeze very well, so make as much as your pot will hold.

tips

- *These are big batches of soup, so try to use an extra-large pot.*
- *Use fresh vegetables any-time you can. If you're using frozen or canned vegetables, try to buy good-quality organic brands.*
- *If you like more texture in your soup, reserve a cup or so of the whole beans or corn. Puree the rest, then add the reserved vegetables to the pureed mixture.*

- *Let the soup cool for a few minutes before blending, and only fill your blender halfway full. You'll be tempted to rush – resist! You don't want a mess on your hands.*
- *If you like an extra-silky smooth soup, and don't mind the extra step, push the pureed soup though a fine-mesh sieve.*
- *Put your leftover soup in freezer-proof bags. If you freeze them flat, you can stack them nicely right on top of each other. Be sure they are well sealed before you stack them.*

- *If you have frozen leftover soup and need a quick defrost, just put the bags of frozen soup in a large bowl of very hot water.*
- *When reheating these soups, avoid boiling – heat until just hot.*

STEP	1	2	3	4
TYPE OF SMOOTH SOUP	SAUTÉ SOUP BASE	SIMMER	PUREE IN BLENDER	WHISK + SEASON
asparagus soup with parmesan	To a large pot over medium heat, add: ▸ 3 T. **extra-virgin olive oil** ▸ 2 **onions**, chopped ▸ 3 **shallots**, chopped ▸ 4 cloves **garlic**, chopped Sauté for 5 minutes, or until the onions start to get soft.	Add: ▸ 2 large bunches **asparagus**, chopped into 1-inch pieces ▸ 4 ½ c. **water** or vegetable stock Bring to a boil, then turn down the heat and simmer for 10 minutes, or until the asparagus is starting to get soft but not mushy. Remove from the heat.	Puree well in a blender, in batches (only fill the blender halfway full). Return the soup to the pot. <u>Note</u>: This is one of the soups I prefer silky smooth, so I push it through a fine-mesh sieve after blending.	Whisk in: ▸ ½ c. low-fat **sour cream** ▸ ½ c. freshly grated **Parmesan cheese** Add **s+p** to taste. I use at least 1 T. salt. Garnish with **Homemade Croutons** (page 16).
bright green pea + mint soup	To a large pot over medium heat, add: ▸ 3 T. **extra-virgin olive oil** ▸ 2 **onions**, chopped ▸ 3 **shallots**, chopped ▸ 4 cloves **garlic**, chopped Sauté for 5 minutes, or until the onions start to get soft.	Add: ▸ 6 c. fresh (shelled) or frozen **peas** ▸ 4 ½ c. **water** or vegetable stock Bring to a boil, then turn down the heat and simmer for 10 minutes. Don't boil too long, or the peas will turn a murky green color and lose their pretty brightness. Remove from the heat. Add: ▸ ⅓ c. fresh **mint** ▸ ⅓ c. fresh **basil** leaves	Puree in a blender, in batches (only fill the blender halfway full). Return the soup to the pot.	Whisk in: ▸ ½ c. low-fat **sour cream** ▸ ½ c. freshly grated **Parmesan cheese** ▸ Juice of 1 **lemon** Add **s+p** to taste. I use at least 1 T. salt.

corn, coconut + curry soup	To a large pot over medium heat, add:
	▸ 3 T. **extra-virgin olive oil**
	▸ 2 **onions**, chopped
	▸ 3 **shallots**, chopped
	▸ 4 cloves **garlic**, chopped
	▸ 2 t. **Thai red curry paste**
	Sauté for 5 minutes, or until the onions start to get soft.
		Add:
		▸ 6 c. fresh or frozen **corn** kernels (about 1 ½ lbs.)
		▸ 1 (14-oz.) can light **coconut milk**
		▸ 4 c. **water**
		Bring to a boil, then turn down the heat and simmer for 10 minutes.
		   Remove from the heat.
			Puree in a blender, in batches (only fill the blender halfway full). Return the soup to the pot.	Add **s+p** to taste. I use 2 t. salt and 10 or so cranks of the black pepper mill.
				   Garnish with grated **lime zest** and fresh **cilantro**.

STEP	1	2	3	4
TYPE OF SMOOTH SOUP	**SAUTÉ SOUP BASE**	**SIMMER**	**PUREE IN BLENDER**	**WHISK + SEASON**
creamy tomato + basil soup	To a large pot over medium heat, add: ▸ 3 T. **extra-virgin olive oil** ▸ 2 **onions**, chopped ▸ 3 **shallots**, chopped ▸ 4 cloves **garlic**, chopped Sauté for 5 minutes, or until the onions start to get soft.	Add: ▸ 8 c. chopped fresh **tomatoes** (about 4 lbs.) ▸ 2 c. **water** or vegetable stock Bring to a boil, then turn down the heat and simmer for 10 minutes. Remove from the heat.	Puree in a blender, in batches (only fill the blender halfway full). Return the soup to the pot.	Whisk in: ▸ 1 c. low-fat **sour cream** ▸ A squeeze of **lemon juice** Add **s+p** to taste. Garnish with ½ c. slivered fresh **basil** and crumbled **goat cheese**.
red pepper puree soup	To a large pot over medium heat, add: ▸ 3 T. **extra-virgin olive oil** ▸ 2 **onions**, chopped ▸ 3 **shallots**, chopped ▸ 4 cloves **garlic**, chopped Sauté for 5 minutes, or until the onions start to get soft.	Add: ▸ 6 large **red bell peppers** (roasted are great too!), seeded and deveined, cut into 1-inch strips ▸ 4 c. **water** Bring to a boil, then turn down the heat and simmer for 20 minutes, or until the fresh peppers soften up. Remove from the heat.	Puree in a blender in batches (only fill the blender halfway full). Return the soup to the pot.	Whisk in: ▸ 1 c. low-fat **sour cream** ▸ Juice of ½ **lemon** Add **s+p** to taste. For this soup I use 1 T. salt and 10 or so cranks of the pepper mill. Garnish with ½ c. slivered fresh **basil** and a generous amount of crumbled **feta cheese**.
wild mushroom soup	To a large pot over medium heat, add: ▸ 3 T. **extra-virgin olive oil** ▸ 2 **onions**, chopped ▸ 3 **shallots**, chopped ▸ 4 cloves **garlic**, chopped Sauté for 5 minutes, or until the onions start to get soft.	Add: ▸ 6 c. sliced **shiitake**, **morel**, or **porcini mushrooms** (about 1 lb.) Sauté for 4 to 5 minutes, until the mushrooms release their liquid. Add: ▸ 4 c. **milk** (low-fat is fine) ▸ 1 t. **salt** Bring just to a boil, then turn down the heat and simmer for 5 minutes	Puree in a blender, in batches (only fill the blender halfway full). Return to the pot.	Whisk in: ▸ ½ c. low-fat **sour cream** ▸ 1 T. **balsamic vinegar** or sherry wine vinegar ▸ 1 t. **salt** ▸ A pinch or two of freshly ground **pepper** Garnish with **Homemade Croutons** (page 16).

chunky chowders

I'm using the term *chowder* loosely here. Essentially any soup with lots of chunks, texture, and big flavor is fair game for this section. I like to draw on the flavors of different regions for these soups, including elements from Thai and Southwestern cooking, to create delicious and memorable chowders.

A homemade bowl of steaming hot chowder can make anyone feel better. Most of the chowders that follow are hot in flavor as well as temperature, which makes them wonderfully comforting on a chilly night. Full of chunks of everything from potatoes and squash to tofu and beans, these chowders are a meal in themselves.

Get ready to do some chopping. This is one of those sections where the payoff doesn't come easy. There's a bit of prep work involved in these recipes, and plenty of elbow grease, but you'll be making big batches and should have delicious leftovers for days after.

tips

- *Use fresh vegetables whenever you can. If you're using frozen or canned vegetables, try to buy good-quality organic brands.*

- *Chowders like these can make for great fillings in Pocket Tarts (pages 47–50) and Pot Pies (pages 64–67). I just scoop the vegetables and chunks from the soup with a slotted spoon, let most of the liquid drain off, and use them as a flavorful filling.*

- *When reheating these soups, avoid boiling – heat just until hot, especially when using sour cream or yogurt.*
- *These chowders are great to serve in individual sourdough bread bowls. Edible bowls are always a big hit with guests.*

RUSTIC POTATO CHOWDER

STEP	1	2	3
TYPE OF CHOWDER	CREATE BASE	ADD INGREDIENTS + SIMMER	WHISK + SEASON
black bean chowder	To a large pot over medium heat, add: ‣ *3 T. **extra-virgin olive oil*** ‣ *2 **onions**, chopped* ‣ *3 **shallots**, chopped* ‣ *4 cloves **garlic**, chopped* ‣ *1 t. **salt*** *Sauté for 5 minutes, or until the onions start to get soft.*	Add: ‣ *4 (15-oz.) cans **black beans**, drained* ‣ *1 (28-oz.) can **crushed tomatoes*** ‣ *2 c. **orange juice*** ‣ *¾ t. **cayenne pepper*** *Bring to a boil, then simmer for 10 minutes. Remove from the heat.*	Whisk in: ‣ *¼ c. **rum** (optional)* *Season with salt to taste*
curried tofu in coconut milk	To a large pot over medium heat, add: ‣ *4 cloves **garlic**, chopped* ‣ *1 (1 ½-inch) piece **ginger**, peeled and grated* ‣ *2 T. **peanut oil*** ‣ *2 t. **Thai red curry paste*** *Sauté just until the garlic is soft, 2 to 3 minutes.*	Add: ‣ *1 (12-oz.) package extra-firm **tofu**, cut into 1/2-inch cubes* ‣ *2 (14-oz.) cans **coconut milk** (light is fine)* ‣ *8 **green onions**, including some of the greens* ‣ *1 T. chopped **lemongrass** (tender hearts of about 3 stalks; optional)* ‣ *3 T. **soy sauce***	Whisk in: ‣ *½ c. **basil**, slivered* *For an added touch of green, I sometimes throw in a bit of broccoli or a couple handfuls of snow peas and simmer until tender.*
rustic potato chowder	To a large pot, cook 8 to 10 slices **fake bacon** according to the package instructions, until browned and crisp. Cool and chop into small pieces. Set aside. In the same pot over medium-high heat, add: ‣ *3 T. **extra-virgin olive oil*** ‣ *2 **onions**, chopped* ‣ *3 **shallots**, chopped* ‣ *4 cloves **garlic**, chopped* *Sauté for 5 minutes, or until the onions start to get soft.*	Add: ‣ *4 c. diced unpeeled **new potatoes**, any color (¼-inch dice)* ‣ *1 t. **salt*** *Sauté for about 2 minutes, then add:* ‣ *1 T. **Dijon mustard*** ‣ *4 c. **milk** (low-fat is fine)* *Bring to a boil, then simmer for about 25 minutes, or until the soup thickens and the potatoes are soft throughout.*	Whisk in: ‣ *1 c. grated **Gruyère cheese**, (optional)* ‣ *Another 1 t. **salt*** ‣ *A couple pinches of freshly ground **pepper*** *Garnish with the fake bacon, fresh **chives**, and/or **chive flowers**.*

STEP	1	2	3
TYPE OF CHOWDER	CREATE BASE	ADD INGREDIENTS + SIMMER	WHISK + SEASON
spicy corn chowder	To a large pot, cook 8 to 10 slices *fake bacon* according to the package instructions, until browned and crisp. Cool and cut into small pieces. Set aside. In the same pot over medium-high heat, add: ‣ 3 T. **extra-virgin olive oil** ‣ 2 **onions**, chopped ‣ 3 **shallots**, chopped ‣ 4 cloves **garlic**, chopped Sauté for 5 minutes, or until the onions start to get soft.	Add: ‣ 6 c. **corn** kernels, fresh or frozen ‣ 2 medium **tomatoes**, chopped ‣ 4 c. **milk** (low-fat is fine) ‣ 1 ½ T. **adobo sauce** (from a can of chipotle chiles) Bring to a boil, then simmer for 10 minutes. Remove from the heat.	Whisk in: ‣ 1 c. low-fat **sour cream** ‣ Fake bacon ‣ 1 ½ t. **salt**, or more to taste ‣ ½ c. slivered fresh **basil**
tomato + chickpea chowder	To a large pot, cook 6 to 8 slices *fake bacon* according to the package instructions, until browned and crisp. Cool and cut into small pieces. Set aside. In the same pot over medium-high heat, add: ‣ 3 T. **extra-virgin olive oil** ‣ ¾ t. ground **cumin** ‣ ½ t. **cayenne pepper** Sauté for about 30 seconds, then add: ‣ 2 **onions**, chopped ‣ 3 **shallots**, chopped ‣ 4 cloves **garlic**, chopped Sauté for 5 minutes, or until the onions start to get soft.	Add: ‣ 2 (14-oz.) cans **diced tomatoes** ‣ 2 (15-oz.) cans **chickpeas**, drained ‣ 2 ½ c. **water** Simmer for about 20 minutes.	Whisk in: ‣ 1 c. **sour cream** (optional; low-fat is fine) ‣ Grated zest of 1 **lemon** ‣ 2 t. **salt**, or more to taste Garnish with the fake bacon.

mashed potatoes SERVES 6 TO 8 GENEROUSLY

Everyone loves a big scoop of creamy, warm mashed potatoes, and no one more than me. As I was growing up, my
dad would often whip up a giant batch for me, my sister,
and any friends who happened to be over. Since we were
kids, no skins and minimal lumps secured his reign as
favorite dad on the block.

Lumpy or smooth, skins or no skins, you can use this
chapter as a starting point. Don't be afraid to try a few different approaches after you find your groove: Mix and
match your favorite flavors and ingredients to find just the
right combination.

POTATO CHOICES If you like your mashed potatoes
light and fluffy, use high-starch russet or Burbank

potatoes. If you like them denser, smoother, and creamier,
opt for the smaller, lower-starch potatoes: Yukon gold,
Yellow Finn, red, or fingerling varieties.

DAIRY AND BUTTER CHOICES You have a bunch of
options here. I usually go the low-fat route for the needed
milk or cream and don't feel like I'm sacrificing too much in
the way of texture and richness. Some people swear by
heavy cream, whole milk, half-and-half, or buttermilk for
richer taste and creamier texture. I usually use 1% low-fat
milk. As far as the butter goes, I use unsalted full-fat butter,
but I use less of it than most mashed potato recipes call for.

tips

- *Leave the skins on regular potatoes, peel sweet potatoes, and cut out any eyes on all types of potatoes.*
- *Cut the potatoes into 1-inch cubes before you boil them.*
- *Boil the potatoes until they're soft all the way through but not totally falling apart.*
- *After you drain your potatoes, dump them back in the pot and leave them over low heat for a few more minutes to dry them out a bit.*

- *If you have the time, make sure all the ingredients you're going to add are at room temperature and not cold.*
- *When it comes to mashing, some people swear by a kitchen tool called a potato ricer. It has an odd shape and ends up being one more thing that takes me forever to wash. Instead, I just use a simple hand potato masher.*

- *Using the food processor to mash your potatoes is a bad idea, unless you like them with the consistency of library paste.*
- *For another variation and significant difference in flavor, try substituting olive oil for the butter.*

SIDES / MASHED POTATOES COOK 1.0 **103**

STEP	1	2	3
TYPE OF MASHED POTATOES	BOIL POTATOES	DRAIN POTATOES + MASH	SEASON AND SERVE
best basic mashed potatoes	To a large pot of boiling water, add: ‣ 4 lbs. Yukon gold or small **yellow potatoes**, washed and cut into 1-inch chunks Cook until soft throughout but not falling apart, about 35 minutes.	Drain well and return the potatoes to the pot. Mash together with: ‣ 1 ⅓ c. **milk** ‣ 5 T. **unsalted butter** ‣ 2 ½ t. **salt** ‣ ¼ t. freshly ground **pepper**	Season again with s+p to taste.
chipotle mashed potatoes	To a large pot of boiling water, add: ‣ 4 lbs. **red potatoes**, washed and cut into 1-inch chunks Cook until soft throughout but not falling apart, about 35 minutes.	Drain well and return the potatoes to the pot. Mash together with: ‣ 1 ⅓ c. **milk** ‣ 5 T. **unsalted butter** ‣ 1 c. grated **white cheddar cheese** ‣ 2 t. **adobo sauce** from a can of chipotle peppers ‣ 2 ½ t. **salt** ‣ ¼ t. freshly ground **pepper**	Season again with s+p to taste.
goat cheese + basil mashed potatoes	To a large pot of boiling water, add: ‣ 4 lbs. **red potatoes**, washed and cut into 1-inch chunks Cook until soft throughout but not falling apart, about 35 minutes.	Drain well and return the potatoes to the pot. Mash together with: ‣ 1 ⅓ c. **milk** ‣ 5 T. **unsalted butter** ‣ 1 c. crumbled **goat cheese** ‣ 2 ½ t. **salt** ‣ ¼ t. freshly ground **pepper**	Season again with s+p to taste. Just before serving, mix in: ‣ 1 c. fresh **basil**, slivered.
lemon + chive mashed potatoes	To a large pot of boiling water, add: ‣ 4 lbs. **russet potatoes**, washed and cut into 1-inch chunks Cook until soft throughout but not falling apart, about 35 minutes.	Drain well and return the potatoes to the pot. Mash together with: ‣ 1 ⅓ c. **milk** ‣ 5 T. **unsalted butter** ‣ Grated zest of 2 **lemons** ‣ Cloves of 1 head **Roasted Garlic** (page 16) ‣ 2 ½ t. **salt** ‣ ¼ t. freshly ground **pepper**	Season again with s+p to taste. Just before serving, mix in: ‣ ¾ c. fresh snipped **chives**

STEP	1	2	3
TYPE OF MASHED POTATOES	BOIL POTATOES	DRAIN POTATOES + MASH	SEASON AND SERVE
mashed sweet potatoes with feta + chives	To a large pot of boiling water, add: ▸ 4 lbs. **sweet potatoes**, washed, peeled, and cut into 1-inch chunks Cook until soft throughout but not falling apart, about 35 minutes.	Drain well and return the sweet potatoes to the pot. Mash together with: ▸ 5 T. **unsalted butter** ▸ 1 c. crumbled **feta cheese** ▸ 2 T. **extra-virgin olive oil** ▸ 2 ½ t. **salt** ▸ ¼ t. freshly ground **pepper**	Just before serving, mix in: ▸ ¾ c. chopped fresh **chives** Season again with s+p to taste.
mashed sweet potatoes with lime + cilantro	To a large pot of boiling water, add: ▸ 4 lbs. **sweet potatoes**, washed, peeled, and cut into 1-inch chunks Cook until soft throughout but not falling apart, about 35 minutes.	Drain well and return the sweet potatoes to the pot. Mash together with: ▸ 5 T. **unsalted butter** ▸ 2 T. **extra-virgin olive oil** ▸ 2 ½ t. **salt** ▸ ¼ t. freshly ground **pepper**	Just before serving, mix in: ▸ 1 c. fresh **cilantro**, chopped ▸ 2 T. fresh **lime** juice ▸ Grated zest of 1 **lime** Season again with s+p to taste.
saffron mashed potatoes	To a large pot of boiling water, add: ▸ 4 lbs. Yukon gold or small **yellow potatoes**, washed and cut into 1-inch chunks Cook until soft throughout but not falling apart, about 35 minutes.	Drain well and return the potatoes to the pot. Mash together with: ▸ 1 ⅓ c. **milk** ▸ 5 T. **unsalted butter**, melted and combined with a pinch of **saffron** threads ▸ 2 ½ t. **salt** ▸ ¼ t. freshly ground **pepper**	Season again with s+p to taste.
ultra roasted garlic mashed potatoes	To a large pot of boiling water, add: ▸ 4 lbs. **russet potatoes**, washed and cut into 1-inch chunks Cook until soft throughout but not falling apart, about 35 minutes.	Drain well and return the potatoes to the pot. Mash together with: ▸ 1 ⅓ c. **milk** ▸ 5 T. **unsalted butter** ▸ Cloves from 2 heads **Roasted Garlic** (page 16) ▸ 2 ½ t. **salt** ▸ ¼ t. freshly ground **pepper**	Season again with s+p to taste.

roasted vegetables

Roasting is very similar to grilling, in that high heat helps give the vegetables a magically rich, concentrated flavor. With roasting you get a nice golden crust on the outside and a tender inside. My very favorite roasted vegetables become wonderfully sweet from the natural sugars inside – winter squashes and sweet potatoes are perfect examples.

Part of the reason I love roasted vegetables is because they're simple, yet they really are the essence of good food. They don't need much in the way of fancy sauces or rubs, and the natural flavors are simply amazing. You can roast just about any vegetable. Prep it, give it a little toss in some oil, and you're all set.

The following recipes focus primarily on my favorite roasted vegetables, the ones I cook most often. Whenever I pull something roasting from the oven and taste it, I regret that I don't roast more often. It's easy and delicious, and an added bonus is that you aren't draining away any nutrients the way you do when you boil vegetables and pour out the water.

While the actual roasting process may take some time, if you put the vegetables in the oven early, they'll roast while you're making the rest of your meal – just check in on them and give them a toss every now and then. Simple. The majority of vegetables will take from 20 minutes to 1 hour to roast.

Roast as many or as few vegetables as you please; the recipe chart lists suggested quantities.

tips

- *Try to start with room temperature vegetables.*
- *If you are in a crunch for time, cut your vegetables smaller and thinner. They will roast more quickly.*
- *If you're roasting more than one kind of vegetable, try to make sure they're similar in size so they'll cook at a comparable rate. If you do have varying sizes of vegetables, group each vegetable type together so you can easily remove each kind as they finish roasting.*

- *Try to use metal roasting pans or baking sheets, not glass. I don't have much luck getting the golden caramelization when I use glass.*
- *Whenever possible, keep the vegetables in a single layer. You will get that nice browning and caramelization wherever the vegetables have touched the pan.*

- *When testing for doneness, try your largest vegetable; it's going to take the longest to cook, so if it's tender throughout, the rest should be fine as well.*

STEP	1	2	3
TYPE OF ROASTED VEGETABLE	PREP VEGETABLES	TOSS + SEASON	ROAST IN OVEN
asparagus	Preheat oven to 400°F. In cold water, rinse and then dry 2 bunches medium-thick **asparagus**. (If you're using pencil-thin asparagus, just reduce the roasting time and keep a close eye on it.) Snap off the woody, tough bottom of each stalk. I never bother to peel them.	Toss with: ▸ 3 T. **extra-virgin olive oil** ▸ 8 cloves **garlic**, peeled and smashed ▸ ¼ t. **salt** ▸ ⅛ t. freshly ground **pepper**	In a roasting pan or rimmed baking sheet, spread asparagus out into a single layer. Roast in the center of the oven for 8 to 10 minutes, depending on the thickness of your spears. When done, the asparagus should be a bit tender, but slightly firm. If it's mushy, you've roasted too long. Remove from the oven and sprinkle with a bit of freshly grated **Parmesan cheese** and/or **lemon zest**.
carrots	Preheat oven to 400°F. Start with: ▸ 10 whole medium **carrots** (about 1 lb.) Give them a good scrubbing to get any soil off them. If the green tops are still on, snip those off as well. Dry well.	Rub with: ▸ 1 T. **extra-virgin olive oil** ▸ A good shake of both **s+p**	In a roasting pan or rimmed baking sheet, spread the carrots out into a single layer. Roast in the center of the oven, tossing once or twice, until tender, golden, and caramelized, about 40 minutes. Remove from the oven and season with more s+p to taste.
corn	Preheat oven to 400°F. Start with: ▸ 4 to 6 ears **corn**, husks still on For an extra treat, I like to gently peel back some of the husk and insert a few dabs of **flavored butter** (see recipes on pages 119–123) before pulling the husk back up and placing corn in the oven.	No seasoning is necessary at this point.	Place the ears directly on the center rack of the oven. Place a pan below to catch any drippings if you added butter. Roast for 12 minutes. Remove from the oven, let cool for a minute or so, unwrap, and season with **s+p**.

STEP	1	2	3
TYPE OF ROASTED VEGETABLE	PREP VEGETABLES	TOSS + SEASON	ROAST IN OVEN

eggplant	Preheat oven to 400°F.
	Start with:
	▸ 2 medium **eggplants** (1 lb. each)
	With a knife, cut the eggplant into ¾-inch cubes.
		Toss with:
		▸ 3 T. **extra-virgin olive oil**
		▸ ¼ t. **salt**
		▸ ⅛ t. freshly ground **pepper**
		▸ A few cloves **garlic**, smashed (optional)
			Place the eggplant in a roasting pan or rimmed baking sheet.
			   Roast in the center of the oven until golden brown and tender throughout, about 35 minutes, tossing the eggplant a few times while it roasts.
			   Season again with s+p to taste.

new potatoes	Preheat oven to 400°F. Start with: ▸ 8 to 12 **new potatoes** (about 2 lbs.); any small, low-starch red, fingerling, Yellow finn, or Yukon gold potatoes will work Scrub clean and carve out any eyes or blemishes, but don't peel. Cut the potatoes into wedges.	Toss with: ▸ 3 T. **extra-virgin olive oil** ▸ ¼ t. **salt** ▸ ⅛ t. freshly ground **pepper** A few cloves **garlic**, smashed (optional)	Place the potatoes in a roasting pan or rimmed baking sheet. Roast in the center of the oven until golden brown and tender throughout, about 45 minutes, tossing the potatoes a couple times while they roast. Season again with s+p to taste.
onions	Preheat oven to 400°F. Start with: ▸ 4 whole **onions**, peeled and cut into quarters or sixths	Toss with: ▸ 3 T. **extra-virgin olive oil** ▸ ¼ t. **salt** ▸ ⅛ t. freshly ground **pepper** Drizzle with **balsamic vinegar** (optional).	Place the onions in a roasting pan or rimmed baking sheet. Roast in the center of the oven until the onions are browned and tender, about 40 minutes, tossing a few times as they roast. Remove from the oven and let cool a bit.

STEP	1	2	3
TYPE OF ROASTED VEGETABLE	PREP VEGETABLES	TOSS + SEASON	ROAST IN OVEN
portobello mushrooms	Preheat oven to 400°F. Start with: ► 4 large **portobello mushrooms** Brush any dirt off the caps and take off the stems.	Toss with: ► 3 T. **extra-virgin olive oil** ► 3 cloves **garlic**, minced ► ¼ t. **salt** ► ⅛ t. freshly ground **pepper**	Place the mushrooms in a roasting pan or rimmed baking sheet. (The mushrooms expel quite a bit of liquid, so you really do need a rimmed pan for this one.) Roast in the center of the oven, flipping the mushrooms onto their backs halfway through, for 25 minutes. Remove from the oven and season again with s+p. These are amazing sliced thinly onto grilled bread with red peppers and Blue Cheese Butter (page 121).
red peppers	Preheat oven to 400°F. Start with: ► 4 whole **red peppers**	No seasoning is necessary at this point.	Place the peppers in a roasting pan or rimmed baking sheet on their sides. Roast in the center of the oven, rotating regularly, until bubbly, charred, and collapsing, about 45 minutes. Place the peppers in a glass bowl covered with plastic wrap for a few minutes as they come out of the oven; they'll steam and be easy to peel.
sweet potatoes or yams	Preheat oven to 400°F. Start with: ► 3 medium **yams** or sweet potatoes Peel and cut into 1 ½-inch chunks.	Toss with: ► 3 T. **extra-virgin olive oil** ► ¼ t. **salt** ► ⅛ t. freshly ground **pepper** ► ⅛ t. **cayenne pepper**	In a roasting pan or rimmed baking sheet, arrange the yams in a single layer. Roast in the center of the oven, tossing once or twice, until tender throughout, golden, and caramelized, about 45 minutes. Remove from the oven and season again with a bit of salt. Serve drizzled with **Lime-Cilantro Vinaigrette** (page 132).

STEP	1	2	3
TYPE OF ROASTED VEGETABLE	PREP VEGETABLES	TOSS + SEASON	ROAST IN OVEN
tomatillos	*Preheat oven to 450°F.* *Start with:* ▸ *8 medium* **tomatillos** *(about 1 lb.)* *Remove husks and rinse well.*	*Rub with:* ▸ *3 T.* **extra-virgin olive oil**	*In a roasting pan or rimmed baking sheet, arrange tomatillos in a single layer. Roast in the center of the oven, tossing once or twice, until tender throughout and golden, about 20 minutes.* *Remove from the oven and season with a bit of* **s+p.** *Use the roasted tomatillos in Tomatillo Salsa (page 128).*
winter squash	*Preheat oven to 400°F.* *Start with:* ▸ *1* **winter squash**, *such as butternut or acorn, or 1 small pumpkin* *Cut butternut squash into 1-inch-thick rounds; other types of squash work better as rectangles or wedges. You can cut off the peel at this point, but you don't have to. Remove the seeds and fibers.* *(Acorn squash is particularly great – simply cut in half, scoop out the seeds, drizzle a little olive oil all over, and pop it in the oven.)*	*Toss with:* ▸ *3 T.* **extra-virgin olive oil** ▸ *¼ t.* **salt** ▸ *⅛ t. freshly ground* **pepper**	*In a roasting pan or rimmed baking sheet, arrange the squash in a single layer. Roast in the center of the oven, tossing once or twice, until tender throughout, golden, and caramelized, 30 to 60 minutes, depending on the size of the pieces and the type of squash.* *Remove from the oven and season again with a bit of salt.* *Serve drizzled with* **Lime-Cilantro Vinaigrette** *(page 132).*
zucchini	*Preheat oven to 400°F.* *Start with:* ▸ *6 medium* **zucchini** *Give them a good scrub, then cut them into ¾-inch-thick rounds.*	*Toss with:* ▸ *3 T.* **extra-virgin olive oil** ▸ *3 cloves* **garlic**, *minced* ▸ *¼ t.* **salt** ▸ *⅛ t. freshly ground* **pepper**	*In a roasting pan or rimmed baking sheet, arrange the zucchini in a single layer. Roast in the center of the oven, tossing once or twice, until tender throughout and golden, about 40 minutes.* *Remove from the oven and season with a bit of freshly grated* **Parmesan cheese** *, s+p, and* **lemon zest**.

SPREADS, SAUCES + SALSAS

dips / flavored butters / sauces /

salsas / vinaigrettes

dips

MAKES 2 TO 3 CUPS / DOUBLE THESE RECIPES FOR PARTY-SIZED PORTIONS

The vegetable tray with obligatory spinach dip in the center has seen its day. Keep this in mind the next time you throw a party. The good news is you can make something better. Everyone loves dips, and many are crowd pleasers with kids and adults alike. It's remarkable that when you puree a handful of ingredients beyond recognition everyone seems to get less picky.

These dips are quick and easy to throw together. Most come together in about 10 minutes, and taste just as good using low-fat ingredients versus their full-fat counterparts. The dips I make most often fall into two categories: blender dips and chop-and-mash dips. A few of each kind are included here.

IDEAS FOR DIPPING Figuring out what type of dip to make is only half the equation – the other half is choosing what to dunk. Depending on the type of dip you're creating, here are some good ideas: pita wedges, baguette slices, crackers, tortilla chips, breadsticks, and vegetable crudités such as endives, bell peppers, small pattypan squash, celery, jícama, asparagus, cherry tomatoes, and green beans. Good fruits for dipping are those that have some structure, such as apples, pears, and melon slices.

tips

- *If you're serving dip with crudités, keep in mind that the color and texture of many vegetables are improved by blanching before serving. Give them a quick swim (just a minute or two) in a large pot of boiling water – just long enough for them to brighten up, but not long enough for them to lose their bite and get mushy.*

  Immediately after that, dunk them in ice-cold water to stop the cooking process. This works great with asparagus, green beans, broccoli, fiddleheads, and sugar snap peas.

- *It's fun to serve dips in creative serving bowls. Anything from a carved-out acorn or butternut squash to red pepper halves works nicely. Melon and citrus halves are also great because they impart a delicious fragrance and added flavor to dips.*

- *Many of the recipes in this section are ideal for more than just dips. Use them as special spreads on sandwiches, homemade pizzas, and quesadillas.*

STEP	1	2	3
TYPE OF "BLENDED" DIP	PREP + PUREE THE MAIN INGREDIENT	COMBINE INGREDIENTS	ADD FINISHING TOUCHES
artichoke dip	*Preheat oven to 350°F.* *In a blender or food processor, puree:* ▸ *2 (14-oz.) cans well-drained water-packed* **artichokes**	*In a separate medium bowl, whisk together:* ▸ *¾ c. freshly grated* **Parmesan cheese** ▸ *⅔ c. light* **mayonnaise** ▸ *⅔ c. low-fat* **sour cream** ▸ *¼ t* **salt**, *or more to taste* ▸ *⅛ t. freshly ground* **pepper** ▸ *3 large cloves* **garlic**, *minced* ▸ *A shake of* **cayenne pepper** *(optional)* *Stir in the artichoke puree and pour into a medium-small baking dish. Sprinkle the top with:* ▸ *½ c. freshly grated* **Parmesan cheese** *(optional)*	*Bake until heated through and the cheese on top starts to brown, about 40 minutes.* *For a spicier version, replace the sour cream with* **Chipotle Fire Dip** *(see below).*
chipotle fire dip	*In a blender or food processor, puree:* ▸ *1 (7-oz.) can* **chipotle chiles** *in adobo sauce*	*In a separate medium bowl, whisk together:* ▸ *1 (16-oz.) container low-fat* **sour cream** ▸ *1 ½ T. of the chipotle puree* *Freeze the leftover chipotle puree for a future use.*	*Great with chips or vegetables, and as a spread on quesadillas.*
hummus	*In a blender or food processor, puree:* ▸ *2 (15-oz.) cans* **garbanzo beans**, *drained* ▸ *Juice of 1* **lemon** ▸ *2 T.* **tahini** ▸ *2 cloves* **garlic** ▸ *1 small handful toasted* **pine nuts** *(see page 16)* ▸ *3 pinches of* **salt** *While blending, add:* ▸ *2 T.* **extra-virgin olive oil** ▸ *¼ c. warm* **water**, *or enough to yield the consistency of a thick milkshake*	▸ ▸ ▸	*Season to taste with more salt and lemon juice.* *I like to double this recipe; my blender can handle up to 4 cans of garbanzos. It's also great to add a bit of cayenne pepper before blending.* *Hummus is a natural fit with toasted pita bread wedges and crisp vegetables, and is delicious garnished with kalamata olives and feta cheese.*

STEP	1	2	3
TYPE OF "BLENDED" DIP	PREP + PUREE THE MAIN INGREDIENT	COMBINE INGREDIENTS	ADD FINISHING TOUCHES
red lentil dip	Rinse 1 ½ c. **red lentils**. Put them in a small saucepan with enough water to cover them by 2 inches. Bring to a simmer over medium heat and cook for 12 minutes, or until the lentils are a bit mushy, and soft throughout. Drain. In a blender or food processor, puree the lentils with: ▸ 2 T. **extra-virgin olive** ▸ ⅓ c. warm **water** ▸ ½ c. crumbled **feta cheese** ▸ Juice of 1 **lemon** ▸ 1 clove **garlic** (optional)	Transfer to a mixing bowl and stir in: ▸ 1 t. **paprika** ▸ ½ t. **cayenne pepper** ▸ ¼ t. **salt**	This is another dip that's a natural pair for toasted pita bread. It's an equally good fit with fresh tortilla chips or chunks of baguette.
roasted red pepper dip	In a blender or food processor, puree: ▸ 8 **Roasted Red Peppers** (page 110), veins and seeds removed (about 1 c. puree)	In a separate medium bowl, whisk together: ▸ ⅔ c. freshly grated **Parmesan cheese** ▸ 1 (16-oz.) container low-fat **sour cream** ▸ 2 pinches of **salt**, or to taste Whisk in the red pepper puree and serve.	This is great with vegetable crudités, toasted pita bread, and baguettes, and works well as a topping or spread on veggie burgers and panini.
tapenade	In a blender or food processor, puree to a chunky texture: ▸ 2 ½ c. Mediterranean-style **olives** (sometimes I use niçoise, other times kalamata, or even a mix of different types – usually whatever is on hand) ▸ 1 T. **capers**, drained (optional), or more to taste ▸ Grated zest of 1 **lemon** ▸ 3 T. **extra-virgin olive oil**	▸ ▸ ▸	You can switch it up a bit by adding orange zest instead of lemon. Or for more heat, add red-pepper flakes. When serving, I like to sprinkle the tapenade with a generous handful of toasted pine nuts (see page 16). Tapenade is great on breadsticks or toasted baguettes, or as a spread on sandwiches.

STEP	1	2	3
TYPE OF "CHOP + MASH" DIP	CHOP + PREP INGREDIENTS	MASH + STIR	ADD FINISHING TOUCHES
guacamole	Set aside: ▸ ½ medium red or white **onion**, finely chopped ▸ 2 cloves **garlic**, chopped ▸ Juice of 1 **lemon** or lime	In a medium bowl, mash (with a fork): ▸ Flesh of 4 large **avocados** (ripe so that when you push on the skin it gives a bit) Stir in the onion, garlic, and lemon juice. Add: ▸ ½ t. **salt** ▸ ⅛ t. freshly ground **pepper**	Adjust s+p to taste. Serve at room temperature with tortilla chips or fresh Homemade Tortillas (page 44).
spicy peanut dip	Set aside: ▸ 2 cloves **garlic**, minced ▸ 4 **green onions**, white parts only, thinly sliced ▸ ½ t. **red-pepper flakes** ▸ 1 T. **soy sauce** ▸ ¾ c. warm **water**	In a medium-sized bowl, mash (with a fork): ▸ 1 c. chunky **peanut butter** Stir in the garlic, green onions, red-pepper flakes, and soy sauce. Gradually stir in the water. Stir well to incorporate.	This is the perfect dip for tiny precooked tortellini and vegetable sticks. It's also great tossed with noodles (you may want to thin it out with a bit more warm water).
sun-dried tomato dip	Set aside: ▸ 1 ½ c. **sun-dried tomatoes** (marinated in oil), drained and minced ▸ 2 cloves **garlic**, minced	In a medium bowl, mash (with a fork) the sun-dried tomatoes and garlic together with: ▸ ½ t. **salt** ▸ 1 (16-oz.) container **sour cream** (low-fat is fine)	Another great quesadilla spread, this is also a good dip for vegetable crudités and toasted pita bread.
white bean dip	Set aside: ▸ ½ c. freshly grated **Parmesan cheese** ▸ 2 cloves **garlic**, minced ▸ Juice of 1 **lemon** ▸ 3 T. **extra-virgin olive oil**	In a medium bowl, mash (with a fork): ▸ 2 (15-oz.) cans **cannellini beans**, drained Stir in the cheese, garlic, lemon juice, and olive oil. Season with: ▸ ½ t. **salt** ▸ ⅛ t. freshly ground **pepper**	Drizzle with **Pesto Sauce** (page 126). This is also good served warm.

flavored butters MAKES 1 CUP

Flavored butter is fast to make, freezer friendly, and it adds that little something special to your dishes. It's also a great place to start experimenting with flavors, in part because the ingredients are cheap and come in small quantities, but also because you're not investing much time if you mess it up.

You can create a flavored butter out of just about anything. Included here are some classics as well as a few recent favorite discoveries. Keep a couple of batches on hand in the refrigerator or freezer and you can add a dollop of Blue Cheese Butter to your warm mashed potatoes, put a sliver of Red Pepper + Gorgonzola Butter on your favorite panini, or add Pineapple Butter to a warm piece of freshly baked Hawaiian bread. The ideas are endless. The next time you think about throwing out leftover basil or cilantro, chop it up and use it in your butter.

THE RIGHT KIND OF BUTTER There are lots of different kinds of butter on the market these days. I recommend buying the freshest, best-quality unsalted butter you can find. If you have a hard time spending $6 for four sticks of butter, don't sweat it. Buy the best you can, as long as it's not margarine (it will change the taste).

PICK YOUR FLAVORS The flavor combinations you can make here are endless. You can make butters that are sweet, savory, spicy, or fruity. Have fun with the ingredients you have around the house and take note of your favorites. Make extra so you always have some on hand for that impromptu brunch or day at the beach.

tips

- *If you have the time, bring all your ingredients to room temperature before mixing them together. It helps keep everything smooth and creamy.*

- *As you're dreaming up your own flavors, keep in mind that the stronger each element, the better. Weak flavors equal weak-tasting butter. Think super-sweet preserves, extra-spicy chili powders, or even juice reductions or concentrate.*

- *Splurge on the best-quality ingredients you can find. If you're using herbs, make sure they're fresh and fragrant. No dried herbs, please! They just don't have the same effect.*

- *For the best blend, let your butter soften, and slice it into smaller pieces before trying to mix in the ingredients.*

- *Keep your flavored butters refrigerated, and immediately freeze any that you know you won't use in the next few days.*

- *A little flavored butter goes a long way. You don't need to use much to get that punch of flavor.*

STEP	1	2	3
TYPE OF BUTTER	PREP THE BUTTER	ADD FLAVORING INGREDIENTS	SERVE OR REFRIGERATE OR FREEZE
anything green herb butter	In a medium bowl, mix: ▸ 1 c. (2 sticks) **unsalted butter**, at room temperature Stir vigorously for a few seconds, until the butter is creamy and soft.	Add: ▸ ⅔ c. mixed chopped fresh herbs such as **tarragon**, **chives**, **basil**, **mint**, and/or **parsley** Stir until well incorporated. Add **salt** to taste.	Use in place of butter on your hot Best Basic Mashed Potatoes (page 104).
basil butter	In a medium bowl, mix: ▸ 1 c. (2 sticks) **unsalted butter**, at room temperature Stir vigorously for a few seconds, until the butter is creamy and soft.	Add: ▸ ⅔ c. chopped fresh **basil** Stir until well incorporated. Add salt to taste.	This is perfect on a big oven-roasted baked potato or grilled corn.
blackberry butter	In a medium bowl, mix: ▸ 1 c. (2 sticks) **unsalted butter**, at room temperature Stir vigorously for a few seconds, until the butter is creamy and soft.	Add: ▸ ⅔ c. **blackberry preserves** Stir until well incorporated.	This is wonderful on hot biscuits (pages 26–29) and scones.
blue cheese butter	In a medium bowl, mix: ▸ 1 c. (2 sticks) **unsalted butter**, at room temperature Stir vigorously for a few seconds, until the butter is creamy and soft.	Add: ▸ 1 c. crumbled **blue cheese** Stir until well incorporated.	Add a dollop to a bowl of piping-hot, creamy polenta.
brown sugar butter	In a medium bowl, mix: ▸ 1 c. (2 sticks) **unsalted butter**, at room temperature Stir vigorously for a few seconds, until the butter is creamy and soft.	Add: ▸ ⅓ c. **brown sugar** ▸ Seeds from 1 **vanilla bean** Stir until well incorporated.	This sweet butter is perfect on Pumpkin-Walnut Pancakes (page 33), waffles, and warm scones.

STEP	1	2	3
TYPE OF BUTTER	PREP THE BUTTER	ADD FLAVORING INGREDIENTS	SERVE OR REFRIGERATE OR FREEZE
honey-lime butter	In a medium bowl, mix: ▸ 1 c. (2 sticks) **unsalted butter**, at room temperature. Stir vigorously for a few seconds, until the butter is creamy and soft.	Add: ▸ ⅔ c. **honey** ▸ Grated zest of 1 or 2 **limes** Stir until the honey is well incorporated.	This is perfect on oven-fresh cornbread or any of the biscuits (see recipes on pages 26–29).
lemon, garlic + chive butter	In a medium bowl, mix: ▸ 1 c. (2 sticks) **unsalted butter**, at room temperature. Stir vigorously for a few seconds, until the butter is creamy and soft.	Add: ▸ ½ c. chopped fresh **chives** ▸ 10 cloves **garlic**, pressed or minced ▸ 1 T. **lemon zest**, or more to taste Stir until well incorporated. Add **salt** to taste.	My all-time favorite flavored butter, I use this in place of garlic butter on bread. It's also wonderful on Basic Drop Biscuits (page 28) and Best Basic Mashed Potatoes (page 104).
mango-curry butter	In a medium bowl, mix: ▸ 1 c. (2 sticks) **unsalted butter**, at room temperature Stir vigorously for a few seconds, until the butter is creamy and soft.	Add: ▸ ½ to ⅔ **mango**, diced (about ⅔ c.) ▸ 1 t. **curry powder** Stir until well incorporated.	Serve with hot Homemade Tortillas (page 44) or naan.
olive-mustard butter	In a medium bowl, mix: ▸ 1 c. (2 sticks) **unsalted butter**, at room temperature Stir vigorously for a few seconds, until the butter is creamy and soft.	Add: ▸ ½ c. chopped pitted **kalamata olives** ▸ 3 T. **Dijon mustard** Stir until well incorporated. Add **salt** to taste.	Use in place of regular butter on Best Basic Mashed Potatoes (page 104).

STEP	1	2	3
TYPE OF BUTTER	PREP THE BUTTER	ADD FLAVORING INGREDIENTS	SERVE OR REFRIGERATE OR FREEZE
pineapple butter	In a medium bowl, mix: ▸ 1 c. (2 sticks) **unsalted butter**, at room temperature Stir vigorously for a few seconds, until the butter is creamy and soft.	Add: ▸ ½ c. **pineapple preserves** or chopped fresh pineapple chunks Stir until well incorporated.	This is terrific on Hawaiian sweet bread. Many grocery stores sell a good mix for your bread machine or you can buy it ready-made.
pistachio butter	In a medium bowl, mix: ▸ 1 c. (2 sticks) **unsalted butter**, at room temperature. Stir vigorously for a few seconds, until the butter is creamy and soft.	Add: ▸ 1 c. crushed shelled **pistachio nuts** Stir until well incorporated. Add **salt** to taste.	This is another great butter to use to add a fresh twist to Best Basic Mashed Potatoes (page 104).
red pepper + gorgonzola butter	In a medium bowl, mix: ▸ 1 c. (2 sticks) **unsalted butter**, at room temperature. Stir vigorously for a few seconds, until the butter is creamy and soft.	Add: ▸ 1 c. crumbled **gorgonzola cheese** ▸ ⅓ c. pureed **red peppers** or Roasted Red Peppers (page 110) Stir until well incorporated. Add **s+p** to taste.	This is wonderful spread on a toasted baguette topped with grilled portobello mushrooms.
toasted pine nut + kalamata olive butter	In a medium bowl, mix: ▸ 1 c. (2 sticks) **unsalted butter**, at room temperature. Stir vigorously for a few seconds, until the butter is creamy and soft.	Add: ▸ ¼ c. chopped toasted **pine nuts** (see page 16) ▸ ¼ c. chopped pitted **kalamata olives** Stir until well incorporated. Add **salt** to taste.	I like to use a bit of this on fresh hot pasta, with grated Parmesan cheese.

sauces REFER TO THE RECIPE CHART FOR YIELDS

Sauces. Encyclopedic volumes are written about them — the theories, the traditions, the pairings, and the ingredients. We're going to keep it pretty simple and straightforward here.

In the most basic terms, a sauce is any flavorful liquid that you add to food to enhance and enrich flavor, add moisture, or, in some cases, add a different texture. It can be thick like an alfredo or enchilada sauce, or as thin and simple as an herb-infused butter.

The following is essentially a collection of my favorite everyday sauce recipes, the ones I use most often. Unlike all the other chapters in this book, there aren't strong ties among them in terms of method, yields, or types of ingredients. They are simply the sauces I make most often.

Some sauces, like pesto, are very strong and flavorful and are used in relatively small quantities to add a punch of flavor and intensity to a dish. You might use quite a bit less of it in comparison to, say, the Bright Red Tomato Sauce; for this reason, the amount of sauce each recipe makes is included in the chart. I've also included sauces that are good for more than one use. I use the Red Pepper Sauce or the Pesto Sauce on everything from sandwiches to pizzas. The Sautéed Mushroom Sauce is delicious over rice or potatoes.

tips

- *Reheat sauces over low heat, and don't let them boil. This will keep most sauces from breaking, and it will keep the sauces with dairy ingredients (like yogurt or sour cream) from curdling.*

- *Add a boost to sauces by throwing in a sprinkling of your favorite fresh herbs just before serving. Fresh basil is a natural addition to tomato sauce, for example, and tarragon tastes great in mushroom sauce.*

- *Double up on sauce recipes and keep leftovers on hand for quick and easy impromptu meals or snacks.*

BRIGHT RED TOMATO SAUCE

STEP	1	2	3
TYPE OF SAUCE	SAUTÉ BASE	COMBINE INGREDIENTS	SEASON + SERVE
bright red tomato sauce *makes about 3 ½ c.*	To a medium saucepan over medium-high heat, add: ▸ 2 T. **extra-virgin olive oil** ▸ 1 t. **red-pepper flakes** ▸ 3 cloves **garlic**, minced ▸ ½ t. **salt** *Sauté until the garlic is just golden, 2 to 3 minutes.*	Stir in: ▸ 1 (28-oz.) can **crushed tomatoes** *Reduce the heat to medium and bring to a simmer; cook for 5 to 10 minutes.*	Add a bit more salt to taste. This is my very favorite simple red sauce, and it takes just a few minutes to make. I use it on pizzas, pastas, and sometimes in soups.
pesto sauce *makes about ¾ c.*	No sauté; this is a blender sauce.	In a blender or food processor, puree: ▸ 2 ½ c. fresh **basil** ▸ ¼ c. toasted **pine nuts** (see page 16) ▸ ⅓ c. freshly grated **Parmesan cheese** ▸ 2 cloves **garlic** ▸ ½ c. **extra-virgin olive oil**	Season with a pinch of **salt** and a squeeze of **lemon juice** to keep it bright. Serve on pasta or as a dip, as a spread on crostini, or sandwiches, or as a sauce on pizzas.
red pepper sauce *makes about 2 c.*	No sauté; this is a blender sauce.	In a blender or food processor, puree: ▸ 2 c. **Roasted Red Peppers** (page 110) ▸ 1 t. **red-pepper flakes** ▸ 3 cloves **garlic** ▸ 1 c. **heavy cream**	Season with **s+p** to taste. Serve on appetizers, or sandwiches, or drizzled over grilled vegetables.
sautéed mushroom sauce *makes about 2 c.*	To a medium saucepan over medium-high heat, add: ▸ A splash of **extra-virgin olive oil** ▸ 2 cloves **garlic**, minced ▸ 3 **shallots**, thinly sliced *Sauté for about 1 minute, until the shallots are a bit soft.*	Stir in 4 c. sliced **mushrooms**. Sauté until the mushrooms are tender, 4 to 5 minutes. Stir in ½ c. **dry Marsala**. Sauté for 5 to 10 minutes, until all the liquids evaporate. Add: ▸ 1 c. **water** or vegetable stock ▸ ½ to 1 c. **heavy cream** *Bring back to a simmer, then remove from the heat.*	Season with **s+p** to taste. Serve on wide-ribboned or baked pasta, or drizzled over rice or potatoes.

salsas MAKES 3 TO 4 CUPS

Salsa livens up all kinds of food. Fortunately, Americans no longer think of salsa as just a topping for tacos, burritos, and quesadillas — or something to have on a tortilla chip. Put savory, spicy salsas on everything from eggs and rice to soups and potatoes, and put sweet salsas on pancakes, waffles, sandwiches, and crêpes.

I use traditional ingredients like tomatoes and tomatillos in many of my salsas, but I also like to explore other ingredients. I've used everything from corn and herbs, beans, and fresh fruit.

I like quite a bit of heat in my salsa, and lots of flavor. If you're worried about your salsa being too hot, add the chiles a little at a time and taste as you go. Most of these recipes are chunky, chopped-typed salsas, but there is one blender recipe for a thinner Tomatillo Salsa, which is great splashed on tacos, eggs, and many roasted vegetables.

tips

- *Keep an eye out for deep red vine-ripened tomatoes. Too often I see salsas made from hard, underripe, slightly green tomatoes. Ripe tomatoes are much more flavorful and look beautiful and appetizing.*

- *Tomatoes have a lot of liquid in them. To avoid a watery salsa, seed the tomatoes before chopping them.*
- *Unless a blender is called for, chop your salsa ingredients by hand. This lends a beautiful rustic texture to the end result.*

- *As with Vinaigrettes (pages 130–133), if you let your salsa sit out at room temperature for an hour or so before serving, the flavors will come together nicely.*

SPREADS, SAUCES + SALSAS / SALSAS COOK 1.0 **127**

STEP	1	2
TYPE OF SALSA	PREP INGREDIENTS	COMBINE + SERVE
avocado salsa	Set aside: ▸ 4 medium-large **tomatillos**, husked, rinsed, loosely chopped, then pureed ▸ 1 **serrano chile**, chopped ▸ ½ **onion**, chopped ▸ Juice of 1 **lime** ▸ **Edible flowers**	In a medium serving bowl, gently combine the tomatillos, chile, onion, and lime juice. Just before you're going to eat, toss in: ▸ 4 **avocados**, chopped into ½-inch dice ▸ 2 big pinches of **salt** Sprinkle with the petals of the edible flowers.
salsa fresca	Set aside: ▸ 4 ripe, medium-large **tomatoes**, diced and seeded (about 1 lb.) ▸ ¼ c. chopped fresh **cilantro** ▸ 1 large clove **garlic**, minced ▸ ½ **onion**, chopped ▸ 1 **serrano chile**, chopped ▸ ½ t. **salt**	In a medium serving bowl, gently combine the tomatoes, cilantro, garlic, onion, chile, and salt. Season again with salt to taste. Let sit for a couple hours before eating so the flavors have a chance to meld.
tomatillo salsa (salsa verde)	Set aside: ▸ 6 to 10 **tomatillos** (about 1 lb.), husked, washed, and cut into quarters (You can also use roasted tomatillos here) ▸ 3 cloves **garlic** (again, roasted is great if you have it on hand) ▸ ¼ c. chopped fresh **cilantro** ▸ 1 **serrano chile**, seeded and finely chopped ▸ ½ **onion**, chopped ▸ ½ t. **salt**	Puree all the ingredients in a blender or food processor. Season again with salt to taste. Let sit for a couple of hours before eating so the flavors have a chance to meld.
tropical pineapple salsa	Set aside: ▸ ½ to 1 medium **pineapple**, cut into ¼-inch pieces (about 2 c.) ▸ ½ **red onion**, chopped ▸ 1 (½-inch) piece **ginger**, peeled and grated ▸ ½ **red bell pepper**, seeded, deveined, and chopped ▸ 1 T. chopped fresh **cilantro** ▸ 1 tiny **red chile**, minced ▸ ⅛ t. **salt**	In a medium serving bowl, gently combine all the ingredients. Season again with salt to taste. Let sit for a couple hours before eating so the flavors have a chance to meld. If you want to add some serious heat to this salsa, add a bit of diced habanero, which goes well with the sweetness of the pineapple.

AVOCADO SALSA

vinaigrettes MAKES 1 ½ CUPS

Sunset at Stinson Beach with a handful of friends, a hot BBQ, ice-cold beer, and some freshly grilled asparagus with a splash of lemony vinaigrette is one of the best ways I can think of to spend a warm California evening. Vinaigrettes are great to have on hand, a breeze to make, and can be much more healthful and flavorful than their supermarket counterparts. Splash them on salads, kabobs, vegetables, fresh-baked bread – their versatility is endless.

A classic vinaigrette recipe typically consists of a ratio of three or four parts oil to one part vinegar. There are countless variations on the flavors you can incorporate.

tips

- *Use the best-quality ingredients you can get your hands on. Stock up on good extra-virgin olive oil and a few high-end vinegars.*
- *To cut some of the oil in these recipes, experiment with whisking in other liquids – jams, yogurts, preserves, or juices.*
- *Make extra. Double or triple these vinaigrette recipes, because they keep well in the refrigerator.*
- *Vinaigrettes solidify when kept in the refrigerator, so give them some time at room temperature to loosen up before dressing a salad.*
- *Use a whisk if you have one – it makes blending (and emulsifying) the vinaigrette easier.*
- *Let the finished vinaigrette sit for a couple hours before serving, either in the refrigerator or on the counter. This allows the flavors to really meld together.*

BASIC FRENCH VINAIGRETTE

STEP	1	2	3	4
TYPE OF VINAIGRETTE	PREP INGREDIENTS	ADD VINEGAR OR CITRUS JUICE	ADD OIL + SEASON	SERVE
basic balsamic vinaigrette	In a medium bowl, combine: ▸ 2 T. *Dijon mustard* ▸ 1 T. *sugar* ▸ 4 cloves *garlic*, *minced*	Whisk in: ▸ ⅓ c. *balsamic vinegar*	Whisk in: ▸ 1 c. *extra-virgin olive oil* ▸ 3 pinches of *salt*	This is great with mixed greens and/or baby spinach, or drizzled over vegetables before roasting.
basic french vinaigrette	To a medium bowl, add: ▸ 2 T. *Dijon mustard*	Whisk in: ▸ ⅓ c. *white wine vinegar*	Whisk in: ▸ 1 c. *extra-virgin olive oil* ▸ A pinch of both *s+p*	This is great with mixed greens and/or baby greens, or drizzled over blanched green beans.
blood orange vinaigrette	In a medium bowl, combine: ▸ 2 *shallots*, *minced* ▸ 1 T. *sugar* ▸ Grated zest and juice of 2 *blood oranges*	Whisk in: ▸ ⅓ c. *white wine vinegar*	Whisk in: ▸ 1 c. *extra-virgin olive oil* ▸ About 3 pinches of *salt*	This is great with grilled asparagus, sprinkled with grated pecorino cheese.
citrus-parmesan vinaigrette	In a medium bowl, combine: ▸ ⅓ c. freshly grated *Parmesan cheese* ▸ Grated zest and juice of 2 *oranges* ▸ 2 T. chopped *shallots*	Whisk in: ▸ 2 T. *white wine vinegar*	Whisk in: ▸ 1 c. *extra-virgin olive oil* ▸ 2 pinches of both *s+p*	This is great with mixed greens, baby greens, and/or butter lettuce, or tossed with hunks of mozzarella and toasted walnuts (see page 16).
cranberry-mustard vinaigrette	In a blender or food processor, puree: ▸ 2 T. chopped *red onion* ▸ 3 T. *sugar* ▸ 1 T. *Dijon mustard* ▸ ⅓ c. *cranberries* (fresh or frozen)	Whisk in: ▸ ⅓ c. *balsamic vinegar*	Whisk in: ▸ 1 c. *canola oil* or olive oil ▸ 3 pinches of *salt*	This is great with mixed greens with walnuts and blue cheese.

STEP	1	2	3	4
TYPE OF VINAIGRETTE	PREP INGREDIENTS	ADD VINEGAR OR CITRUS JUICE	ADD OIL + SEASON	SERVE
fresh herb vinaigrette	In a blender or food processor, puree: ‣ 2 **shallots** ‣ ½ c. fresh **basil** ‣ ½ c. fresh **mint**	Whisk in: ‣ ¼ c. fresh **lemon juice**	Whisk in: ‣ 1 c. **extra-virgin olive oil** ‣ 3 pinches of **salt** ‣ 1 pinch of freshly ground **pepper**	This is great drizzled over kabobs and oven-roasted vegetables. I like to make this in the blender or food processor, where it gets nice and creamy, but you don't have to; if you just mince all the ingredients, it comes out just as tasty.
grapefruit-champagne vinaigrette	In a medium bowl, combine: ‣ 2 **shallots**, minced ‣ 2 T. fresh **grapefruit juice**	Whisk in: ‣ 2 T. **champagne vinegar**	Whisk in: ‣ 1 c. **extra-virgin olive oil** ‣ 2 T. **walnut oil** ‣ 2 **grapefruit** segments, ripped into pieces ‣ 3 pinches of **salt**	This is great with mixed greens, baby greens, and/or butter lettuce.
lemon-goat cheese vinaigrette	To a medium bowl, add: ‣ 2 **shallots**, minced	Whisk in: ‣ Grated zest and juice of 1 **lemon**	Whisk in: ‣ 1 c. **extra-virgin olive oil** ‣ ⅓ c. crumbled **goat cheese** ‣ A couple pinches of both **s+p**	This is great with mixed greens, baby greens, and/or grilled asparagus.
lime-cilantro vinaigrette	In a medium bowl, combine: ‣ ¼ c. chopped cilantro ‣ 2 cloves **garlic**, minced	Whisk in: ‣ Grated zest and juice of 3 **limes**	Whisk in: ‣ 1 c. **extra-virgin olive oil** ‣ 2 generous pinches of both **s+p**	This is great drizzled around Mashed Sweet Potatoes with Feta + Chives (page 105).

STEP	1	2	3	4
TYPE OF VINAIGRETTE	PREP INGREDIENTS	ADD VINEGAR OR CITRUS JUICE	ADD OIL + SEASON	SERVE
mint-orange vinaigrette	In a medium bowl, combine: ▸ ¼ c. slivered fresh **mint** ▸ 2 cloves **garlic**, minced	Whisk in: ▸ Grated zest and juice of 2 **oranges**	Whisk in: ▸ ¼ c. **walnut oil** ▸ ¾ c. **extra-virgin olive oil** ▸ 2 to 3 **orange** segments, torn into small pieces ▸ 3 pinches of **salt**	This is great with butter lettuce. If you want a creamier texture, give this one a quick whirl in a blender or food processor.
pome-granate vinaigrette	In a medium bowl, combine: ▸ ½ c. **pomegranate seeds** and any residual juice ▸ 2 T. **sugar**	Whisk in: ▸ ⅓ c. **balsamic vinegar**	Whisk in: ▸ 1 c. **canola oil** or olive oil ▸ 3 pinches of **salt**	This is great with mixed greens and nuts, and also makes a terrific holiday dressing.
red pepper vinaigrette	In a blender or food processor, puree: ▸ ⅓ c. **Roasted Red Peppers** (page 110)	Whisk in: ▸ 3 T. **white wine vinegar**	Whisk in: ▸ 1 c. **extra-virgin olive oil** ▸ 3 pinches of **salt** ▸ 1 pinch of freshly ground **pepper**	This is great on a panini with grilled portobello mushrooms and gorgonzola, or a pizza, in place of the sauce; or drizzle over roasted vegetables or kabobs.
roasted garlic vinaigrette	In a blender or food processor, puree: ▸ 5 large cloves **Roasted Garlic** (page 16) ▸ 1 T. **Dijon mustard**	Whisk in: ▸ ¼ c. **white wine vinegar**	Whisk in: ▸ 1 c. **extra-virgin olive oil** ▸ ¼ cup freshly grated **Parmesan cheese** ▸ 3 pinches of **salt**	This is great with Best Basic Mashed Potatoes (page 104), in place of the butter.

SWEETS

shortcakes / tarts /
sherbets / vanilla gelato with toppings /
tuiles / cobblers

shortcakes MAKES 6 INDIVIDUAL SHORTCAKES

When I think of all-American desserts, shortcake comes second only to apple pie. An authentic shortcake is created by spooning fresh, uncooked fruit over a split, warm, rich, tender biscuit. A couple billowy dollops of whipped cream are added to complete this dreamy treat. The biscuits start to soak up the wonderfully sweet syrupy juices oozing from the fruit, and the chilled clouds of cream contrast with the oven-fresh warmth of the freshly baked biscuits. Heavenly.

Since there are only three major components to a shortcake (the biscuit, the fruit, and the cream), it's important to get the biscuits right. While the Basic Drop Biscuit recipe (page 28) will work fine as is, I like to add just a bit of sugar to the flour in the beginning to sweeten them up. This creates a slightly sweeter and crustier shortcake biscuit. You can roll and stamp the biscuits into uniform shapes before baking, or use the quicker drop biscuit method. Drop the biscuit mixture onto the baking sheet in small mounds, giving each one a custom-made one-of-a-kind perfectly imperfect shape.

Biscuits, the cake in shortcakes, cobbler tops, and scones are all very closely related. All use similar ingredients and baking methods. If you can make one, you should have no trouble making them all.

tips
- *Don't even think about using frozen fruit for shortcakes. The fruit you use needs to be fresh and juicy.*
- *When deciding on fruit, you want to think soft, sweet, and ripe. Because the fruit used in a shortcake recipe is uncooked, you can't get away with firm, crisp fruits like pears, apples, or peaches.*
- *For an added bit of sweetness and crunch, brush biscuits with a light coating of egg white and a sprinkling of sugar before placing them in the oven.*

STEP	1	2	3
TYPE OF SHORTCAKE	MAKE FRUIT FILLING	MAKE BISCUITS	WHIP CREAM + SERVE
classic strawberry shortcake	Start with: ▸ 2 baskets ripe **strawberries**, washed, hulled, and thinly sliced ▸ ¼ c. **sugar** Puree half of the strawberries with the sugar. Stir in the remaining berries and set aside.	Make **Basic Drop Biscuits** (page 28), sifting ¼ cup **sugar** in with the flour mixture to sweeten them up a bit. You'll use 6 of the biscuits for this shortcake.	In a clean, chilled, medium bowl, whisk: ▸ 1 ½ c. **heavy cream** ▸ 2 T. **sugar** Beat until soft billowy peaks form. 　Split the biscuits in half. Divide the fruit among the bottom half of each of the 6 biscuits. On top of the fruit, dollop a generous amount of whipped cream. Put tops of the biscuits back on over the whipped cream and dollop with a bit more whipped cream. Serve immediately.
mixed berry shortcake	Start with: ▸ 1 small basket of each of the following: **strawberries**, **blackberries**, and **raspberries** ▸ ¼ c. **sugar** Gently rinse the berries, and thinly slice the strawberries. Puree half of the strawberries and raspberries with the sugar. Stir in the remaining berries and set aside.	Make **Basic Drop Biscuits** (page 28), sifting ¼ cup **sugar** in with the flour mixture to sweeten them up a bit. You'll use 6 of the biscuits for this shortcake.	In a clean, chilled, medium bowl, whisk: ▸ 1 ½ c. **heavy cream** ▸ 2 T. **sugar** Beat until soft billowy peaks form. 　Split the biscuits in half. Divide the fruit among the bottom half of each of the 6 biscuits. On top of the fruit, dollop a generous amount of whipped cream. Put the tops of the biscuits back on over the whipped cream and dollop with a bit more whipped cream. Serve immediately.
tropical shortcake	Start with: ▸ ½ to 1 medium **pineapple**, cored and cut into ½-inch chunks (about 2 c.) ▸ 1 **mango**, diced (about 1 c.) ▸ 3 T. **sugar** Puree half of the pineapple and half of the mango with the sugar. Stir in the remaining pineapple and mango. Set aside.	Make **Citrus Biscuits** (page 28), sifting ¼ cup sugar in with the flour to sweeten them up a bit. You'll use 6 of the biscuits for this shortcake	In a clean, chilled, medium bowl, whisk: ▸ 1½ c. **heavy cream** ▸ 2 T. **sugar** ▸ ½ t. peeled grated fresh **ginger** Beat until soft billowy peaks form. 　Split the biscuits in half. Divide the fruit among the bottom half of each of the 6 biscuits. On top of the fruit, dollop a generous amount of whipped cream. Put the tops of the biscuits back on over the whipped cream and dollop with a bit more whipped cream. 　Sprinkle with ½ c. **Toasted Coconut Flakes** (page 16) and serve immediately.

tarts MAKES 1 (9 1/2-INCH) TART

Fruit tarts seem very fancy with their fanned fruit and glazes, but they're quite simple to pull together. Making tarts is similar in spirit to making a pie – you just use a slightly different pan (particularly if you're using pastry dough instead of the pat-in-pan crusts we're going to use).

I was determined to simplify the way I'd made tarts in the past. I wanted a delicious, rustic-yet-sophisticated tart without the fuss or extra time required when using pastry dough or pastry creams. What I ended up with is a tart method that takes roughly 15 minutes or so of active time (the rest of the time the tart is either in the oven or setting), and gives me the flexibility of using whatever seasonal fruits I have on hand. The flavor of each fruit (or, in one case, chocolate) is able to shine through against a sweet cookie crust. It's great to serve tarts like these in place of cakes at parties, lunches, showers, picnics, and during holidays – anywhere you'd expect to find a group of sweet tooths.

PAT-IN-PAN CRUSTS If you are up for a low-maintenance crust, this method is for you. Think two-minute crust, and you're on the right track. No more rolling out pastry dough, or waiting for the unbaked crust to chill in the fridge. These crusts are sweet, structured, and rarely get soggy or soft. They're beautiful served in the pan, or gently coaxed out and set on your favorite serving board.

The concept here is simple: Mix finely crumbled cookies, graham crackers, or shortbread with melted butter to form a sandy crumble. Then gently press an even layer into the tart pan. Bake, cool, and fill. Couldn't be easier.

APRICOT AND BERRY GLAZES Glazes help to make your fruit tart shiny and pretty, as if you just brought it home from the bakery. They also help keep your tarts a bit moist – you don't want your fruit to dry out.

I make glazes out of just about any kind of jam, but I use apricot and berry most often. For each 1/4 cup **jam**, add about 2 tablespoons **warm water** to thin it out a bit. Gently brush this mixture across the top of the fruit tart with a pastry brush. I usually try to match the color and flavor with whatever fruit I'm using: berry jam glaze on berry tarts, apricot jam glaze on lighter-color fruits (so you don't end up staining them all berry color).

tips

- *When making a fruit tart, use the very best fruit you can find. I avoid frozen fruit because it seems to steam in the oven from all the extra moisture and condensation, even after it has thawed.*
- *I've found that pie weights are important, even with the pat-in-pan crusts. When I don't use them, the tart shells shrink down from the rim of the tart pan quite a bit. If you don't have pie weights on hand, after you pat your crust in place, place a sheet of aluminum foil on top and fill it with a cup or two of dried beans, then place it in the oven.*
- *Bake tart shells on a baking sheet; this makes it easier to take them out of the oven without crumbling and ruining the edges of the crust. A bonus for tarts with baked fillings is that if your tart bubbles over, you'll have saved yourself the cleanup.*
- *The baked tarts are perfect served warm out of the oven. Serve them with a side of creamy cold vanilla ice cream flecked with vanilla beans, or a dollop of Sweetened Fresh Whipped Cream (page 16).*
- *I love smaller tarts. Not necessarily the bite-sized ones – more like the ones made in 6- or 7-inch pans. The same goes for cakes. Very cute. Because most people have 9- or 10-inch pans, I decided to go with the more standard size for these recipes. If you want a cuter tart, play around with some slightly smaller, nonstandard-sized pans.*

RASPBERRY TART

STEP	1	2	3
TYPE OF TART	MAKE CRUST	PREPARE FILLING + ASSEMBLE TART	MAKE GLAZE + FINISH TART
apple tart	Preheat oven to 375°F. In a food processor, place: ▸ 3 ¼ c. crumbled **gingersnaps** ▸ ⅓ c. **brown sugar** ▸ 6 T. **unsalted butter**, melted Pulse until the mixture is a sandy, grainy texture. Press the crumb mixture into the bottom and up the sides of a 9 ½ -inch tart pan. Add pie weights if you have them. Bake for 10 minutes. Remove from the oven, remove the weights, and let cool to room temperature.	Prep 4 medium-sized firm, tart **apples** such as Granny Smith: Core them and cut them in half lengthwise. Slice very thinly lengthwise. Keep the slices stacked like a deck of cards. Arrange the apples in the crust, either in a circular pattern starting wide and working your way in, or in columns (which is easier and takes less time). Lay down the slices as if you were fanning a deck of cards. Use all the apples; it's okay if they fill the crust quite full. Sprinkle the tart with ¼ c. **sugar**. Mix 1 t. **cinnamon** into the sugar if you like.	Gently place the tart on the center rack of the oven and bake for 25 minutes, or until the apples are golden and starting to get soft. Remove from the oven and set on a rack to cool a bit. Use a pastry brush to coat the tart with **apricot glaze** (page 139). Serve warm or at room temperature.
apricot summer tart with macadamia shortbread crust	Preheat oven to 375°F. In a food processor, place: ▸ 3 c. crumbled **shortbread** or sugar cookies ▸ ⅓ c. **sugar** ▸ ¼ c. **macadamia nuts**, chopped ▸ 6 T. **unsalted butter**, melted Pulse until the mixture is a sandy, grainy texture. Press the crumb mixture into the bottom and up the sides of a 9 ½-inch tart pan. Add pie weights if you have them. Bake for 10 minutes. Remove from the oven, remove the weights, and let cool to room temperature.	Prep 1 ¼ lbs. unpeeled **apricots** or peaches: Cut them in half and remove pits. If you're using peaches, cut them into eighths. Arrange the apricots in the tart crust. I just toss them in the crust, then fuss with them a bit until they look nice, or you can arrange them pitted side up, in a circular pattern starting wide and working your way in (cradling). Sprinkle the tart with ¼ c. sugar.	Gently place the tart on the center rack of the oven and bake for 40 to 45 minutes, until the apricots are just beginning to get golden. Remove from the oven and set on a rack to cool a bit. Use a pastry brush to coat the tart with **apricot glaze** (page 139). Serve warm or at room temperature.

STEP	1	2	3
TYPE OF TART	MAKE CRUST	PREPARE FILLING + ASSEMBLE TART	MAKE GLAZE + FINISH TART
cherry tart with hazelnut shortbread crust	Preheat oven to 375°F. In a food processor, place: <ul><li>3 c. crumbled **shortbread** or sugar cookies</li><li>⅓ c. **sugar**</li><li>6 T. **unsalted butter**, melted</li><li>¼ c. **hazelnuts**</li></ul> Pulse until the mixture is a sandy, grainy texture. Press the crumb mixture into the bottom and up the sides of a 9 ½-inch tart pan. Add pie weights if you have them. Bake for 10 minutes. Remove from the oven, remove the weights, and let cool to room temperature.	Prep 1 ½ lbs. ripe **cherries**: Wash, dry, stem, and pit them. Arrange the cherries in the crust in a circular pattern. Sprinkle the tart with ¼ c. sugar.	Gently place the tart on the center rack of the oven and bake for 40 minutes, until the cherries are soft. Remove from the oven and set on a rack to cool a bit. Use a pastry brush to coat the tart with apricot glaze (page 139). Serve warm or at room temperature.
midnight chocolate tart	Preheat oven to 375°F. In a food processor, place: <ul><li>3 ¼ c. crumbled **chocolate wafer cookies**</li><li>⅓ c. **sugar**</li><li>6 T. **unsalted butter**, melted</li></ul> Pulse until the mixture is a sandy, grainy texture. Press the crumb mixture into the bottom and up the sides of a 9 ½-inch tart pan. Add pie weights if you have them. Bake for 10 minutes. Remove from the oven, remove the weights, and let cool to room temperature.	In a saucepan over medium heat, place: <ul><li>1 ½ c. **heavy cream**</li><li>1 T. fine-ground **espresso coffee beans**</li></ul> Bring to a boil, then immediately add: <ul><li>12 oz. premium-quality **semisweet chocolate**, cut into small chunks</li></ul> Remove from the heat. Stir until the chocolate is melted and fully integrated into the cream. Let cool for 10 minutes or so before filling the tart shell. Slowly pour the chocolate into the crust and chill in the refrigerator for a few hours or overnight, until the chocolate sets.	Garnish with perfectly fresh **red raspberries**, or a dollop of **Sweetened Fresh Whipped Cream** (page 16) and serve cool.

STEP	1	2	3
TYPE OF TART	MAKE CRUST	PREPARE FILLING + ASSEMBLE TART	MAKE GLAZE + FINISH TART
raspberry tart	Preheat oven to 375°F. In a food processor, place: ▸ 3 ¼ c. crumbled **shortbread** or sugar cookies ▸ ⅓ c. **sugar** ▸ 6 T. **unsalted butter**, melted Pulse until the mixture is a sandy, grainy texture. 　Press the crumb mixture into the bottom and up the sides of a 9 ½-inch tart pan. Add pie weights if you have them. Bake for 10 minutes. Remove from the oven, remove the weights, and let cool to room temperature.	In a small bowl, beat: ▸ 1 c. **mascarpone** or cream cheese, at room temperature ▸ ⅓ c. sugar Spread the mixture evenly over the crust. 　Prep 2 to 3 baskets **raspberries**: Rinse and dry them well. (You can also do a mix of berries. I like to use raspberries, strawberry halves, and blueberries.) 　Arrange the berries in the crust in a circular pattern, stem side down, starting wide and working your way in, laying the berries in rows of concentric circles until the crust is full.	Use a pastry brush to coat the tart with **berry glaze** (page 139) or dust with powdered sugar. Serve chilled or, as I prefer, at room temperature.
rustic plum tart	Preheat oven to 375°F. In a food processor, place: ▸ 3 ¼ c. crumbled **shortbread** or sugar cookies ▸ ⅓ c. **sugar** ▸ 6 T. **unsalted butter**, melted Pulse until the mixture is a sandy, grainy texture. 　Press the crumb mixture into the bottom and up the sides of a 9 ½-inch tart pan. Add pie weights if you have them. Bake for 10 minutes. Remove from the oven, remove the weights, and let cool to room temperature.	Prep 10 ripe **plums**: Wash them and then cut into eighths. 　Arrange the plums in the shell. I just toss them in the pan, and then fuss with them a bit until they look nice. 　Sprinkle the tart with ¼ c. sugar.	Gently place the tart on the center rack of the oven and bake for 40 minutes, until the plums are soft, and brown at the edges. 　Remove from the oven and set on a rack to cool a bit. 　Use a pastry brush to coat the tart with **apricot glaze** (page 139). 　Serve warm or at room temperature.

sherbets MAKES 1 QUART

Lighter than ice cream and creamier than sorbet, sherbets have always topped my list of favorite frozen desserts. Until recently, I had no idea that making sherbets could be so simple. Pop your favorite fruits into a blender, sweeten it up a bit, and you're in business. Fresh fruit, frozen fruit, overripe fruit – it all seems to work.

This is one of those sections where it pays to have those fancy kitchen gadgets hiding away in your cupboards. You're going to need a blender and an electric ice-cream maker for these recipes.

RULE OF THUMB I like pure, single-flavored frozen desserts, but you can mix it up a bit. Just use a total of 4 cups fruit. So, for example, you could use 4 cups strawberries, or 3 cups strawberries and 1 cup mango.

tips

- *Use the ripest fruit you can find. Great fruit will really make a difference in the flavor and consistency of the sherbet.*
- *A splash of alcohol can help keep things even creamier. Fruit-flavored schnapps will work well and gives an added element of flavor. Don't overdo it, though, or you're going to end up with more of a slushy than a sherbet.*
- *If you are using fresh and not frozen fruit, be sure to give it a good wash first. You want to get rid of any pesticide residue that might be clinging to the fruit if you aren't using organic produce.*
- *Some fruits like berries can be too seedy for many peoples' taste, including my own. If your puree happens to be extra seedy, just quickly pour it through a strainer before freezing or pouring into an ice-cream maker, and toss out the seeds. You'll end up with impossibly smooth, light sherbet – without the crunch.*
- *I avoid using the fat-free version of sweetened condensed milk in these recipes. It tends to be less creamy, and the taste of the sherbet is noticeably different.*

FRESHEST BERRY SHERBET

STEP	1	2	3	4
TYPE OF SHERBET	PUREE FRUIT	ADD MILK	FREEZE IN ICE-CREAM MAKER	SERVE
blood orange sherbet	*In a blender, puree:* ► *4 medium-sized* **blood oranges**, *peeled (grate the zest, if you're up for it, and stir it in later). Push the puree through a sieve into a small bowl.*	*Add:* ► *1 (14-oz.) can* **sweetened condensed milk** *Stir until combined.*	*Pour into an ice-cream maker and freeze according to the manufacturer's instructions.*	*Put sherbet in between your favorite thin cookies or Citrus Tuiles (page 152) for a delicious ice-cream sandwich.*
daiquiri sherbet	*In a blender, puree:* ► *1* **banana**, *chopped and frozen (about 1 c.)* ► *1 medium* **pineapple**, *cut into 1-inch pieces and frozen (about 3 c.)*	*Add:* ► *1 (14-oz.) can* **sweetened condensed milk** ► *A splash of* **rum** ► *A squeeze of fresh* **lime** *juice*	*Pour into an ice-cream maker and freeze according to the manufacturer's instructions.*	*This sherbet is great sprinkled with Toasted Coconut Flakes (page 16) or finely chopped crystallized ginger.*
freshest berry sherbet	*In a blender, puree:* ► *4 c. very fresh* **berries** *(make sure they're clean, with no mold; I use strawberries, raspberries, blackberries, or a mixture) Push the puree through a sieve into a small bowl.*	*Add:* ► *1 (14-oz.) can* **sweetened condensed milk**	*Pour into an ice-cream maker and freeze according to the manufacturer's instructions.*	*Make 3 or 4 flavors for a sherbet sampler plate.*

STEP	1	2	3	4
TYPE OF SHERBET	PUREE FRUIT	ADD MILK	FREEZE IN ICE-CREAM MAKER	SERVE
melon sherbet	In a blender, puree: ▶ 1 to 2 super-ripe **melons**, cut into 1-inch pieces and frozen (about 4 c.; I like to use cantaloupe or honeydew)	Add: ▶ 1 (14-oz.) can **sweetened condensed milk**	Pour into an ice-cream maker and freeze according to the manufacturer's instructions.	Keep your orange peels or melon halves intact and use as serving bowls for your sherbet.
peach sherbet	In a blender, puree: ▶ 4 to 5 **peaches**, peeled, sliced, and frozen (about 4 c.) ▶ A splash of **apricot brandy** (1 to 2 capfuls)	Add: ▶ 1 (14-oz.) can **sweetened condensed milk**	Pour into an ice-cream maker and freeze according to the manufacturer's instructions.	Put the sherbet in between your favorite thin cookies or Coconut Tuiles (page 154) for a delicious ice-cream sandwich.
strawberry-vodka sherbet	In a blender, puree: ▶ 4 c. **strawberries**, frozen ▶ A splash of **vodka** (1 to 2 capfuls)	Add: ▶ 1 (14-oz.) can **sweetened condensed milk**	Pour into an ice-cream maker and freeze according to the manufacturer's instructions.	Sprinkle each serving with a few sugared mint leaves. (To sugar mint leaves, brush each leaf with a thin coat of egg white. Dip each leaf in a dish of superfine sugar to coat and let dry.)

vanilla gelato with toppings

I can walk into an ice-cream or gelato shop with a hundred flavors on the board, and if it looks like they have a great vanilla – fresh, creamy, packed with an army of little vanilla flecks – my choice is easy. I'll pick vanilla every time.

In addition to being the perfect complement to warm pies, not to mention piping-hot, oozy chocolate brownies, vanilla gelato can provide a great foundation for a host of slightly more sophisticated toppings. Many of my favorites are listed here.

When convenient, I make my own gelato (see the Simple Vanilla Gelato recipe below), but when I'm in a pinch for time, any high-quality vanilla gelato or ice cream will do.

SIMPLE VANILLA GELATO (MAKES 1 QUART)

I have a hard time enjoying homemade ice cream (with its cup after cup of heavy cream) when I like this recipe just as much, or better. So this is what I make for myself when I'm craving a rich, creamy vanilla. I let my vanilla beans sit in a bottle of vodka all year, so the bean is nice and supple with lots of little vanilla bean flecks waiting to be squeezed out into the pot of milk.

4 c. **whole milk**
1 **vanilla bean**, split open
1 c. **sugar**
3 T. plus 2 t. **cornstarch**
1 t. **vanilla extract**

Place 3 cups of the milk in a small saucepan with the vanilla bean over medium-low heat.

Meanwhile, pour the remaining 1 cup milk into a large glass measuring cup. Add the sugar and the cornstarch. Mix well.

When the milk starts to simmer, remove it from the heat and pour in the cornstarch mixture, stirring the whole time. Return the saucepan to medium-low heat and stir, stir, stir, until things start thickening up, 10 to 12 minutes. It should end up thicker than, say, a runny milkshake, but thinner than a frosty one.

Pour the mixture though a strainer into a mixing bowl, whisk in the vanilla extract, and let it cool on the counter for 20 minutes or so. Put the mixture in the refrigerator for a couple hours, or until completely chilled. Don't skimp here; let it get really cold or you'll end up with runny vanilla gelato. Pour into an ice-cream maker and freeze according to manufacturer's instructions. Serve with toppings.

tips

- *I like to keep gelato and ice-cream toppings simple. I focus on a single ingredient or flavor that will complement the ice cream but not overpower it. Why buy great gelato if you're then going to drown it in every possible sundae topping from your refrigerator door? Restrain yourself, and enjoy a simple ingredient or two with your creamy vanilla.*

- *Let ice cream sit out on the counter for 5 minutes or so before serving – just long enough for it to soften up a bit. It tastes better and is much easier to scoop.*

STEP	1	2	3
TYPE OF VANILLA GELATO	PREP INGREDIENTS	CREATE TOPPING	SERVE
vanilla gelato with balsamic berries	*Prep 1 basket of the best **strawberries** you can find: Rinse, dry, hull, and thinly slice them.* *Combine:* ► *2 T. **balsamic vinegar*** ► *¼ c. **superfine sugar***	*In a small bowl, combine the strawberries and the vinegar mixture. Gently stir, and set it aside until ready to serve.*	*Scoop **Simple Vanilla Gelato** (page 147) into 6 small bowls. Top with the strawberries, and serve immediately.*
vanilla gelato with crushed amaretti	*Lightly crush about 1 ½ c. **Italian amaretti**. Set aside.*	*Measure 6 shots **amaretto** into a glass.*	*Scoop **Simple Vanilla Gelato** (page 147) into 6 small bowls. Drizzle 1 shot of the amaretto across each bowl of gelato. Sprinkle the tops of each bowl with about ¼ c. crushed amaretti. Serve immediately.*
vanilla gelato with crushed cinnamon candies	*Thoroughly crush 1 c. **cinnamon disk-shaped hard candies**.*	*Slowly heat half of the candies in a small saucepan over medium-low heat, just until the candies have melted.*	*Scoop **Simple Vanilla Gelato** (page 147) into 6 small bowls. Drizzle melted cinnamon syrup across the gelato, and sprinkle with the remaining crushed candies. Serve immediately.*
vanilla gelato with espresso	*Brew a single shot of **espresso** for each bowl of ice cream you are making. Set the espresso aside, but keep in mind that you want to do the rest of the steps quickly so the espresso stays hot.*	*If you have the espresso brewed, you're ready to go.*	*Scoop **Simple Vanilla Gelato** (page 147) into 6 small bowls. Drizzle 1 shot of the espresso across each bowl of gelato. Serve immediately or sooner.*

STEP	1	2	3
TYPE OF VANILLA GELATO	PREP INGREDIENTS	CREATE TOPPING	SERVE
vanilla gelato with mint-infused chocolate sauce	*Chop ½ lb. high-quality semi-sweet chocolate.*	*In a medium saucepan, combine:* ▸ *⅓ c. fresh mint leaves* ▸ *1 c. heavy cream* *Place over medium-low heat just until cream starts to simmer. Turn the heat off, cover the pan, and let the cream steep for 10 to 15 minutes.* *Pour through a sieve into a small bowl and discard the mint. Stir in the chocolate and mix until well combined.*	*Scoop Simple Vanilla Gelato (page 147) into 6 small bowls. Drizzle the chocolate over the gelato. Garnish each bowl with 1 or 2 mint leaves, and serve immediately.*
vanilla gelato with tropical toppings	*Set aside:* ▸ *⅔ c. Toasted Coconut Flakes (page 16)* ▸ *⅓ c. crystallized ginger, slivered* ▸ *¾ c. unsalted macadamia nuts, crushed* ▸ *½ medium pineapple, chopped (about 1 ½ c.)*	*In a small bowl, toss together the coconut, ginger, and macadamia nuts.*	*Scoop Simple Vanilla Gelato (page 147) into 6 small bowls. Scoop ¼ c. of the pineapple onto each bowl of gelato. Sprinkle with the coconut mixture and serve immediately.*

tuiles MAKES 24

Tuiles (pronounced "tweels") are thin, crisp cookies. I put them next to the vanilla gelato recipes because this is exactly where they belong – snappy tuiles are perfectly paired with creamy ice cream or gelato, particularly if you're using the tuile as an edible spoon. The word *tuile* is French for "tile": when hot out of the oven, place tuiles over a rounded object (like a rolling pin or baguette mold) so their shape will resemble a curved roof tile when they cool.

I think of tuiles as light, airy, magical fairy food. Using this basic method you can shape them into many different forms and use them in a host of different ways. I love tiny tuile cones filled with mini scoops of gelato, tuile ice-cream sandwiches, and delicious flavored tuiles dipped halfway into dark chocolate.

tips

- *Don't overmix your batter.*
- *Use cardboard templates (sort of like a stencil) to make tuiles of varying shapes and sizes. Set the template on the baking sheet, hold it down firmly, and spread the batter across the template using an off-set spatula. Carefully lift the template with both hands, straight up, so you don't smear your shape.*
- *If you have a silicone baking mat, you should use it for this recipe instead of parchment. It's easier to spread the batter on a silicone mat.*

- *I can't emphasize this enough: Spread your batter extremely thin, or when you put the tuiles in the oven the edges will burn badly before the thicker parts even start cooking.*
- *When these cookies are in the oven you have to watch them like a hawk – they bake in a flash and will burn even faster. Set a timer, tie yourself to the oven, do whatever it takes to hold your attention.*
- *After these cookies come out of the oven, they'll harden fast. Be gentle and work quickly. If they firm up before you have a chance to shape them, just pop them back in the oven for a few seconds to soften up, then try again.*

- *Make ice-cream cones with tuiles as they come out of the oven by wrapping them around a cone or a piece of aluminum foil molded into a cone shape.*
- *Drape tuiles over the bottom of drinking glasses of all sizes to shape cups for custards, ice cream, sherbets, and gelatos. For a wider cup, sandwich a fresh-out-of-the-oven tuile between two stacked bowls.*
- *Tuiles can be stored in an airtight container for a day or two. If you leave them out for more than a few hours, they tend to get soft and lose their crispness.*

STEP	1	2	3
TYPE OF TUILES	PREP INGREDIENTS	MAKE BATTER	FORM TUILES + BAKE
basic tuiles	Preheat oven to 400°F. Set aside: ▸ 6 T. **unsalted butter**, melted and cooled for a couple minutes ▸ ¾ c. **sugar** ▸ ¼ t. **vanilla extract** ▸ 2 large **egg whites** ▸ ⅓ c. **unbleached all-purpose flour** Place a piece of parchment paper or a nonstick baking mat on a cookie sheet.	In a small bowl, stir the butter, sugar, and vanilla together until well combined. 　Add the egg whites and mix until well incorporated. 　Fold in the flour. Mix only as much as necessary to get the flour incorporated into the rest of the batter.	Use a spoon to spread a small circle of tuile batter onto the prepared baking sheet, about 1 t. of batter for each tuile. Spread the batter 3 inches wide with the back of the spoon, moving in swirls to coax the batter into shape. Spread very, very thinly – you should almost be able to see the parchment or baking mat through the batter. 　Bake, in batches, in the middle of the oven for 6 minutes, or until golden. 　Remove from the oven and carefully transfer the tuiles to curl around a rolling pin. Let them cool completely on the pin. Be gentle and work quickly.
citrus tuiles	Preheat oven to 400°F. Set aside: ▸ 6 T. **unsalted butter**, melted and cooled for a couple minutes ▸ ¾ c. **sugar** ▸ Grated zest of 2 **oranges** ▸ ¼ t. **vanilla extract** ▸ 2 large **egg whites** ▸ ⅓ c. **unbleached all-purpose flour** Place a piece of parchment paper or a nonstick baking mat on a cookie sheet.	In a small bowl, stir the butter, sugar, orange zest, and vanilla together until well combined. 　Add the egg whites and mix until well incorporated. 　Fold in the flour. Mix only as much as necessary to get the flour incorporated into the rest of the batter.	Use a spoon to spread a small circle of tuile batter onto the prepared baking sheet, about 1 t. of batter for each tuile. Spread the batter 3 inches wide with the back of the spoon, moving in swirls to coax the batter into shape. Spread very, very thinly – you should almost be able to see the parchment or baking mat through the batter. 　Bake, in batches, in the middle of the oven for 6 minutes, or until golden. 　Remove from the oven and carefully transfer the tuiles to curl around a rolling pin. Let them cool completely on the pin. Be gentle and work quickly.

BASIC TUILES

STEP	1	2	3
TYPE OF TUILES	PREP INGREDIENTS	MAKE BATTER	FORM TUILES + BAKE
coconut tuiles	Preheat oven to 400°F. Set aside: ► 6 T. **unsalted butter**, melted and cooled for a couple minutes ► ¾ c. **sugar** ► ¼ t. **vanilla extract** ► 2 large **egg whites** ► ⅓ c. **unbleached all-purpose flour** ► 1 c. **sweetened coconut flakes** Place a piece of parchment paper or a nonstick baking mat on a cookie sheet.	In a small bowl, stir the butter, sugar, and vanilla together until well combined. Add the egg whites and mix until well incorporated. Fold in the flour. Mix only as much as necessary to get the flour incorporated into the rest of the batter.	Use a spoon to spread a small circle of tuile batter onto the prepared baking sheet, about 1 t. batter for each tuile. Spread the batter 3 inches wide with the back of the spoon, moving in swirls to coax the batter into shape. Spread very, very thinly – you should almost be able to see the parchment or baking mat through the batter. Sprinkle the top of each cookie with a generous pinch of coconut flakes. Bake in batches, in the middle of the oven for 6 minutes, or until golden. Remove from the oven and carefully transfer the tuiles to curl around a rolling pin. Let them cool completely on the pin. Be gentle and work quickly.
espresso tuiles	Preheat oven to 400°F. Set aside: ► 6 T. **unsalted butter**, melted and cooled for a couple minutes ► ¾ c. **sugar** ► 1 T. fine-ground **espresso coffee beans** ► ¼ t. **vanilla extract** ► 2 large **egg whites** ► ⅓ c. **unbleached all-purpose flour** Place a piece of parchment paper or a nonstick baking mat on a cookie sheet.	In a small bowl, stir the butter, sugar, espresso, and vanilla together until well combined. Add the egg whites and mix until well incorporated. Fold in the flour. Mix only as much as necessary to get the flour incorporated into the rest of the batter.	Use a spoon to spread a small circle of tuile batter onto the prepared baking sheet, about 1 t. batter for each tuile. Spread the batter 3 inches wide with the back of the spoon, moving in swirls to coax the batter into shape. Spread very, very thinly – you should almost be able to see the parchment or baking mat through the batter. Bake, in batches, in the middle of the oven for 6 minutes, or until golden. Remove from the oven and carefully transfer the tuiles to curl around a rolling pin. Let them cool completely on the pin. Be gentle and work quickly.

STEP	1	2	3
TYPE OF TUILES	**PREP INGREDIENTS**	**MAKE BATTER**	**FORM TUILES + BAKE**
ginger-snap tuiles	Preheat oven to 400°F. Set aside: ‣ 6 T. **unsalted butter**, melted and cooled for a couple minutes ‣ ¾ c. **sugar** ‣ ⅓ c. **crystallized ginger**, finely minced ‣ 1 (1-inch) piece of fresh **ginger**, peeled and grated ‣ ¼ t. **vanilla extract** ‣ 2 large **egg whites** ‣ ⅓ c. **unbleached all-purpose flour** Place a piece of parchment paper or a nonstick baking mat on a cookie sheet.	In a small bowl, stir the butter, sugar, crystallized ginger, fresh ginger, and vanilla together until well combined. Add the egg whites and mix until well incorporated. Fold in the flour. Mix only as much as necessary to get the flour incorporated into the rest of the batter.	Use a spoon to spread a small circle of tuile batter onto the prepared baking sheet, about 1 t. batter for each tuile. Spread the batter 3 inches wide with the back of the spoon, moving in swirls to coax the batter into shape. Spread very, very thinly – you should almost be able to see the parchment or baking mat through the batter. Bake, in batches, in the middle of the oven for 6 minutes, or until golden. Remove from the oven and carefully transfer the tuiles to curl around a rolling pin. Let them cool completely on the pin. Be gentle and work quickly.
vanilla tuiles	Preheat the oven to 400° F. Set aside: ‣ 6 T. **unsalted butter**, melted and cooled for a couple minutes ‣ ¾ c. **sugar** ‣ Seeds from 2 **vanilla beans** ‣ ¼ t. **vanilla extract** ‣ 2 large **egg whites** ‣ ⅓ c. **unbleached all-purpose flour** ‣ 1 c. **dried cherries**, finely minced (optional) Place a piece of parchment paper or a nonstick baking mat onto a cookie sheet.	In a small bowl, stir the butter, sugar, fresh vanilla, and vanilla extract together until well combined. Add the egg whites and mix until well incorporated. Fold in the flour. Mix only as much as necessary to get the flour incorporated into the rest of the batter.	Use a spoon to spread a small circle of tuile batter onto the prepared baking sheet, about 1 t. batter for each tuile. Spread the batter 3 inches wide with the back of the spoon, moving in swirls to coax the batter into shape. Spread very, very thinly – you should almost be able to see the parchment or baking mat through the batter. Sprinkle the top of each cookie with a touch of the dried cherries. Bake, in batches, in the middle of the oven for 6 minutes, or until golden. Remove from the oven and carefully transfer the tuiles to curl around a rolling pin. Let them cool completely on the pin. Be gentle and work quickly.

cobblers MAKES 1 (8-INCH) COBBLER

I came across a great cobbler maker at a fair in eastern Tennessee. Apparently there are two rules of cobbler making that are not up for discussion: True cobblers must never be round, and they must never have a bottom crust. I admit I sometimes cheat and make individual cobblers in small circular bowls. Of course I lament when I don't get the perfect thick, crisp topping that forms so beautifully in each of the four corners of a square cobbler dish. If you are one of those people who fight for the corner chocolate brownies, you know what I'm talking about. Magical things happen to baked goods when two sides intersect into a corner.

A great all-American family-style dessert, the best cobblers should be juicy, but not soupy, and complemented by a tender, slightly sweet golden-topped biscuit. That's what I'm aiming for here.

tips

- *In most cases it's best to use fresh fruit for these cobblers, but if in a pinch you want to use frozen, just let the fruit thaw out a bit before beginning so the sugar and flour mixture will stick to it better. You may also need to increase the baking time a bit.*

- *To save time, you can prepare the biscuit dough for cobblers up to a few days in advance. Keep the dough covered tightly with plastic wrap in the refrigerator until you're ready to use it.*
- *Don't overdo it. If you make the topping dollops too large they won't cook throughout, and the insides and bottoms will be doughy and soggy.*

- *For an extra-special touch, you can roll out the biscuit dough ½-inch thick and cut it into shapes with large cookie cutters. Lay the cutout shapes on top of the fruit instead of using dollops of biscuit batter.*
- *It's a good idea to bake these over a baking sheet in case the cobbler bubbles over.*

STEP	1	2	3
TYPE OF COBBLER	MAKE FRUIT BASE	MAKE TOPPING	ASSEMBLE + BAKE
classic berry cobbler	Preheat oven to 425°F. In a medium bowl, whisk together: ▸ ¼ c. **sugar** ▸ 1 T. **cornstarch** Add: ▸ 3 ½ c. mixed **berries** (blackberries, raspberries, and blueberries are all great) Toss well and transfer to an 8-inch square baking dish.	In a separate bowl, mix up dough for a single batch of **Basic Drop Biscuits** (page 28), sifting in ¼ c. sugar with the flour to sweeten the dough a bit.	Drop the biscuit dough in walnut-sized dollops onto the fruit mixture, about 12 dollops total. Sprinkle the tops with a small handful of sugar. You'll have extra dough, so save the leftovers for a later use. 　Bake in the middle of the oven until the topping is golden and the juices are bubbling around it, about 25 minutes. 　Serve warm, with the best possible vanilla ice cream you can find, or simply drizzled with fresh cream.
cherry cobbler	Preheat oven to 425°F. In a medium bowl, whisk together: ▸ ¼ c. **sugar** ▸ 1 T. **cornstarch** Add: ▸ 3 ½ c. (about 1 lb.) pitted **cherries** (If you use frozen, make sure they're thawed.) Toss well and transfer to an 8-inch square baking dish.	In a separate bowl, mix up dough for a single batch of **Basic Drop Biscuits** (page 28), sifting in ¼ c. sugar with the flour to sweeten the dough a bit.	Drop the biscuit dough in walnut-sized dollops onto the fruit mixture, about 12 dollops total. Sprinkle the tops with a small handful of sugar. You'll have extra dough, so save the leftovers for a later use. 　Bake in the middle of the oven until the topping is golden and the juices are bubbling around it, about 25 minutes. 　Serve warm, with the best possible vanilla ice cream you can find, or simply drizzled with fresh cream.
cranberry-apple cobbler	Preheat oven to 425° F. In a medium bowl, whisk together: ▸ ½ c. **sugar** ▸ 1 T. **cornstarch** ▸ 1 T. **cinnamon** ▸ ¼ t. freshly grated **nutmeg** Add: ▸ 3 large **apples**, washed, cored, and very thinly sliced (about 4 c.) ▸ 1 c. **cranberries** Toss well and transfer to an 8-inch square baking dish.	In a separate bowl, mix up dough for a single batch of **Basic Drop Biscuits** (page 28), sifting in ¼ c. sugar with the flour to sweeten the dough a bit.	Drop the biscuit dough in walnut-sized dollops onto the fruit mixture, about 12 dollops total. Sprinkle the tops with a small handful of sugar. You'll have extra dough, so save the leftovers for a later use. 　Bake in the middle of the oven until the topping is golden and the juices are bubbling around it, about 25 minutes. 　Serve warm, with the best possible vanilla ice cream you can find, or simply drizzled with fresh cream.

STEP	1	2	3
TYPE OF COBBLER	MAKE FRUIT BASE	MAKE TOPPING	ASSEMBLE + BAKE
peach-blackberry cobbler	Preheat oven to 425°F. In a medium bowl, whisk together: ▸ ¼ c. **sugar** ▸ 1 T. **cornstarch** ▸ Grated zest of 1 **orange** Add: ▸ 3 to 4 **peaches**, unpeeled, washed, dried, pitted, and cut into eighths (about 3 ½ cups) ▸ 1 c. **blackberries** Toss well and transfer to an 8-inch square baking dish.	In a separate bowl, mix up dough for a single batch of **Basic Drop Biscuits** (page 28), sifting in ¼ c. sugar with the flour to sweeten the dough a bit.	Drop the biscuit dough in walnut-sized dollops onto the fruit mixture, about 12 dollops total. Sprinkle the tops with a small handful of sugar. You'll have extra dough, so save the leftovers for a later use. 　Bake in the middle of the oven until the topping is golden and the juices are bubbling around it, about 25 minutes. 　Serve warm, with the best possible vanilla ice cream you can find, or simply drizzled with fresh cream.
pineapple-rum cobbler	Preheat oven to 425°F. In a medium bowl, whisk together: ▸ ¼ c. **dark brown sugar** ▸ 1 T. **cornstarch** Add: ▸ 1 large **pineapple**, cut into ¾-inch chunks (about 3 ½ c.) Toss well and transfer to an 8-inch square baking dish. Drizzle with ¼ c. dark **rum**.	In a separate bowl, mix up dough for a single batch of **Basic Drop Biscuits** (page 28), sifting in ¼ c. sugar with the flour to sweeten the dough a bit.	Drop the biscuit dough in walnut-sized dollops onto the fruit mixture, about 12 dollops total. Sprinkle the tops with a small handful of **sugar**. You'll have extra dough, so save the leftovers for a later use. 　Bake in the middle of the oven until the topping is golden and the juices are bubbling around it, about 25 minutes. 　Serve warm, with the best possible vanilla ice cream you can find, or simply drizzled with fresh cream.
simple raspberry cobbler	Preheat oven to 425°F. In a medium bowl, whisk together: ▸ ¼ c. **sugar** ▸ 1 T. **cornstarch** Add: ▸ 3 ½ c. **raspberries**, gently rinsed and dried ▸ Grated zest of 2 **lemons** Toss well and transfer to an 8-inch square baking dish.	In a separate bowl, mix up dough for a single batch of **Citrus Biscuits** (page 28), sifting in ¼ c. sugar with the flour to sweeten the dough a bit.	Drop the biscuit dough in walnut-sized dollops onto the fruit mixture, about 12 dollops total. Sprinkle the tops with a small handful of sugar. You'll have extra dough, so save the leftovers for a later use. 　Bake in the middle of the oven until the topping is golden and the juices are bubbling around it, about 25 minutes. 　Serve warm, with the best possible vanilla ice cream you can find, or simply drizzled with fresh cream.

DRINKS

spritzers / iced teas / lemonades /
sangrías / margaritas

SPARKLING CITRUS SPRITZER

spritzers MAKES 1 MEDIUM-SIZED PITCHER, ABOUT 1 QUART

Spritzers, sparklers, flavored sparkling water – whatever you want to call them, these quenchers are my favorite daytime beverages. They dance on my tongue, tingle their way down into my stomach, and can refresh me right out of a frumpy postlunch slump. I have to skip any wine-based spritzers during the day because they put me right to sleep.

My love of spritzers probably comes from my love of water – I drink a lot of it, probably close to a gallon a day. Sparkling, still, flavored, vitamin-enriched – I drink them all. I drink sparkling water the way many people drink sodas. The main things to remember about making terrific spritzers are: lots of ice, and good, unsweetened sparkling water.

In addition to tasting great and being the ultimate refresher, spritzers are the kind of simple, fancy nonalcoholic drink everyone needs in their recipe repertoire. Something special, tasty, and pretty to serve to those friends and little ones who aren't imbibing. They're great at showers and brunches, and kids love the colorful fruit suspended among the ice cubes.

tips

- *Serve these in a simple, clear glass pitcher. This way people can see the pretty fruit slices and berries.*

- *Fill your pitcher with ice before adding the sparkling water. I try to fill the pitcher at least three quarters full of ice for starters. Warm sparkling water defeats the purpose.*

- *Give your fruits a good scrub before adding them. Dirt, sand, and bugs have a way of spoiling a nice ice-cold drink.*

STEP	1	2	3
TYPE OF SPRITZER	PREP FRUIT	FILL PITCHER	ADD SPARKLING WATER
sparkling cherry spritzer	*Set aside:* ▸ *1 basket sweet juicy* **cherries***, washed, stemmed, and pitted*	*Fill your nicest medium-sized glass pitcher alternately with the cherries and lots of ice cubes. Take care to make sure the fruit is suspended all throughout the ice.*	*Pour in:* ▸ *1 (1-liter) bottle* **unsweetened sparkling water** *(berry flavor is great if you can find it)* *Serve. Refill the pitcher with more ice and sparkling water as needed.*
sparkling citrus spritzer	*Set aside:* ▸ *1* **lemon***, washed and sliced* ▸ *1* **orange***, washed and sliced*	*Fill your nicest medium-sized glass pitcher alternately with the orange and lemon slices and lots of ice cubes. Take care to make sure the fruit is suspended all throughout the ice.*	*Pour in:* ▸ *1 (1-liter) bottle* **unsweetened sparkling water** *(orange flavor is great if you can find it)* *Serve. Refill the pitcher with more ice and sparkling water as needed.*
sparkling mixed berry spritzer	*Set aside:* ▸ *1 to 2 baskets mixed* **berries***, rinsed, well dried, and then frozen (I like to use a mix of equal parts blueberries, blackberries, strawberries, and raspberries.)*	*Fill your nicest medium-sized glass pitcher alternately with the berries and lots of ice cubes. Take care to make sure the fruit is suspended all throughout the ice.*	*Pour in:* ▸ *1 (1-liter) bottle* **unsweetened sparkling water** *(berry flavor is great if you can find it)* *Serve. Refill the pitcher with more ice and sparkling water as needed.*
sparkling peach spritzer	*Set aside:* ▸ *3* **peaches***, pitted and cut into eighths (I sometimes freeze the slices and use them alongside ice cubes.)*	*Fill your nicest medium-sized glass pitcher alternately with the peach slices and lots of ice cubes. Take care to make sure the fruit is suspended all throughout the ice.*	*Pour in:* ▸ *1 (1-liter) bottle* **unsweetened sparkling water** *Serve. Refill the pitcher with more ice and sparkling water as needed.*
sparkling raspberry-lime spritzer	*Set aside:* ▸ *1 small basket* **raspberries***, rinsed* ▸ *2* **limes***, washed and sliced*	*Fill your nicest medium-sized glass pitcher alternately with the berries, limes, and lots of ice cubes. Take care to make sure the fruit is suspended all throughout the ice.*	*Pour in:* ▸ *1 (1-liter) bottle* **unsweetened sparkling water** *(lime flavor is great if you can find it)* *Serve. Refill the pitcher with more ice and sparkling water as needed.*

iced teas

During certain times of the year, the afternoon sun beating down on the foothills of the Santa Cruz mountains would get so hot that I could smell the redwood planks on our back porch heating up. Homebrewed sun tea was a fixture on that porch. Many summer mornings, my dad would place a few tea bags in a large gallon-sized plastic jug with a small spout at the bottom, fill it with water and a shake of sugar, and walk it out to its rightful place in the sun. As the day went on, the sun would get stronger and the water in the jug would slowly turn from clear to a deep golden brown shade. He would take his frosted mug from the freezer, fill it with fresh ice cubes, and walk out to his sun-tea jug to fill his glass to the rim.

Iced tea, sweet tea, sun tea – it seems like just about every sun-kissed region in America has a variation on this summertime cooler. The sweet teas I had in rural Tennessee were sweet enough to give you a cavity on the spot, and the California sun tea I grew up on had just a kiss of sugar. As far as ingredients go, some people stick strictly to tea bags, while others add fruits and all sorts of flavors.

The following instructions are written as stovetop recipes. You boil your tea bags, add any other ingredients, let the mixture cool, and then chill it in the refrigerator. Some people get a little nervous about brewing sun tea these days, since you may run a slight risk of food poisoning. I still brew sun tea, but I make sure my jug is extra clean and I add anything perishable after the tea comes out of the sun and cools. Place everything in the refrigerator as soon as possible.

I like my iced tea with just a bit of sweetness. If you like your teas sweeter, feel free to boost the amount of sugar, or serve it with a sugar bowl on the side so people can add their own extra sugar.

tips

- *For a while my tea would get a bit cloudy in the refrigerator. I've found that you can keep your tea cloud-free by letting it cool on the counter completely before placing it in the refrigerator.*

- *If your tea bags have strings, tie them together for easy removal.*
- *Use good-quality water for your teas. Run your water through a filter pitcher for an easy solution. If your tap water tastes bad, so will your iced tea.*

- *After your tea is finished simmering and you're going to strain the hot liquid into a large container or jug, place the jug in your sink before attempting to pour. This catches any inevitable spills. Also, having the jug farther below you makes pouring much easier.*

BEST BASIC ICED TEA

STEP	1	2	3
TYPE OF ICED TEA	SIMMER	FILL PITCHER	COOL + SERVE
best basic iced tea	In an extra-large pot or saucepan over medium heat, slowly bring to a boil: ▸ 12 c. *water* ▸ 7 *black tea bags* ▸ 1 *lemon*, sliced ▸ 1 stick *cinnamon* ▸ 1 c. *sugar* As soon as the tea comes to a boil, remove from the heat, cover, and let steep for 5 minutes. The color of the tea should be deep and the sugar should be dissolved.	Fish out the tea bags, lemon slices, and cinnamon stick. Carefully strain into a large jug.	Set the jug, uncovered, on your counter for 1 to 2 hours, until the tea is cool enough to place in the refrigerator. Serve cold, in a frosty glass filled with ice. I like to garnish this iced tea with 1 or 2 slices lemon.
citrus sunshine iced tea	In an extra-large pot or saucepan over medium heat, slowly bring to a boil: ▸ 12 c. *water* ▸ 3 *orange-flavored tea bags* ▸ 4 *lemon-flavored tea bags* ▸ 1 *orange*, washed and sliced ▸ 1 *lemon*, washed and sliced ▸ 1 c. *sugar* As soon as the tea comes to a boil, remove from the heat, cover, and let steep for 5 minutes. The color of the tea should be deep and the sugar should be dissolved.	Fish out the tea bags and orange and lemon slices. Carefully strain into a large jug. Sometimes I leave the fruit slices in if I am going to serve the tea relatively soon.	Set the jug, uncovered, on your counter for 1 to 2 hours, until the tea is cool enough to place in the refrigerator. Serve cold, in a frosty glass filled with ice.
ginger iced tea	In an extra-large pot or saucepan over medium heat, slowly bring to a boil: ▸ 12 c. *water* ▸ 7 *lemon-flavored tea bags* ▸ 1 c. *sugar* ▸ 1 (3-inch) piece *ginger*, peeled, thinly sliced into coin-shaped circles, and smashed a bit As soon as the tea comes to a boil, remove from the heat, cover, and let steep for 5 minutes. The color of the tea should be deep and the sugar should be dissolved.	Fish out the tea bags. Carefully strain into a large jug.	Set the jug, uncovered, on your counter for 1 to 2 hours, until the tea is cool enough to place in the refrigerator. Serve cold, in a frosty glass filled with ice.

STEP	1	2	3
TYPE OF ICED TEA	SIMMER	FILL PITCHER	COOL + SERVE

mint iced tea	In an extra-large pot or saucepan over medium heat, slowly bring to a boil:
	▸ 12 c. **water**
	▸ 7 **orange-flavored tea bags**
	▸ 1 c. **sugar**
	▸ ½ c. smashed **mint** leaves
	As soon as the tea comes to a boil, remove from the heat, cover, and let steep for 5 minutes. The color of the tea should be deep and the sugar should be dissolved.
		Fish out the tea bags.
		   Carefully strain into a large jug.
			Set the jug, uncovered, on your counter for 1 to 2 hours, until the tea is cool enough to place in the refrigerator.
			   Serve cold, in a frosty glass filled with ice.

pome-granate iced tea	In an extra-large pot or saucepan over medium heat, slowly bring to a boil:
	▸ 12 c. **water**
	▸ 7 **berry-flavored tea bags**
	▸ 2 **pomegranates**, seeds and juice only
	▸ 1 c. **sugar**
	As soon as the tea comes to a boil, remove from the heat, cover, and let steep for 5 minutes. The color of the tea should be deep and the sugar should be dissolved.
		Fish out the tea bags.
		   Carefully strain into a large jug.
			Set the jug, uncovered, on your counter for 1 to 2 hours, until the tea is cool enough to place in the refrigerator.
			   Serve cold, in a frosty glass filled with ice.

spiced apple iced tea	In an extra-large pot or saucepan over medium heat, slowly bring to a boil:
	▸ 12 c. **water**
	▸ 7 **spice-flavored tea bags**
	▸ 1 **apple**, washed and cut into ¼-inch wedges
	▸ 1 stick **cinnamon**
	▸ A couple whole **cloves**
	▸ 1 c. **sugar**
	As soon as the tea comes to a boil, remove from the heat, cover, and let steep for 5 minutes. The color of the tea should be deep and the sugar should be dissolved.
		Fish out the tea bags, apple and cinnamon stick.
		   Carefully strain into a large jug.
			Set the jug, uncovered, on your counter for 1 to 2 hours, or until the tea is cool enough to place in the refrigerator.
			   Serve cold, in a frosty glass filled with ice.

lemonades MAKES 1 GIANT JUG OF ICE-COLD REFRESHING LEMONADE, ABOUT 1 GALLON

There is something deeply satisfying about looking at my kitchen counter piled high with a mountain of lemons, a sack of sugar, a big jug, and an old-fashioned juicer. Knowing that after a few minutes of sweat and elbow grease – not to mention stinging lemon juice in any paper cuts I might have – I'll have a delicious, ice-cold jug of fresh homemade lemonade is the perfect reward.

The base lemonade for this chart is a lemonade that's sweet but not too sweet, and tart but not so tart that your lips pucker when you take a sip. It's strong enough to hold up to the bit of dilution that happens when the ice starts to melt in the jug of lemonade.

tips

- *Get the most juice out of your lemons. Start with room temperature lemons and firmly roll them beneath your palm on the kitchen counter before juicing. This will soften the lemons up and make them as juicy as possible.*
- *For picnics and parties, serve up lemonade with a ladle in extra-large, wide-mouthed glass containers like cookie jars, jugs, and preservative jars.*

- *Make a slushy by filling a blender full of ice and lemonade, and any other ingredients, such as berries. Puree until nice and frosty, like you would a blended margarita.*
- *Make sparkling lemonade by substituting sparkling water for the still water.*
- *Not everyone is up for squeezing the juice out of a dozen lemons. Not a problem – just go ahead and buy a good lemonade from the store. Use it as a base and add in any extra ingredients. This is great if you're time pressed but you still want to serve something special.*

- *If you're really up for a challenge, zest all your lemons with a Microplane grater before juicing. Freeze or save the zest in the refrigerator for a quick boost of lemon in future recipes.*
- *If your tap water tastes questionable, use filtered water instead. Poor-tasting water can affect the taste of your lemonade.*
- *I like to use superfine sugar when making lemonade. It dissolves faster and doesn't collect at the bottom of the pitcher as much as regular sugar.*

BASIC BEST HOMEMADE LEMONADE

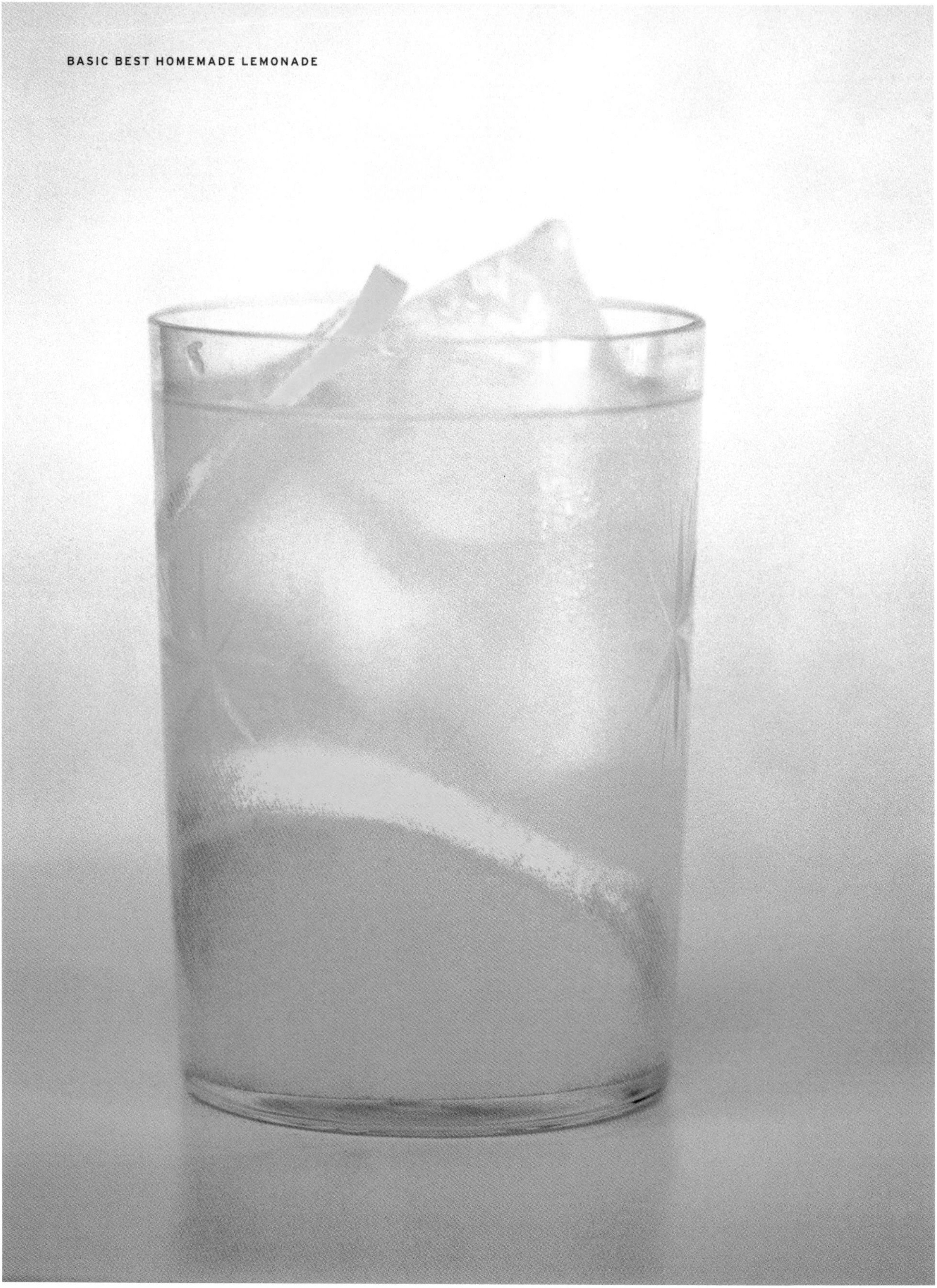

STEP	1	2	3
TYPE OF LEMONADE	JUICE LEMONS	PREP ADDITIONAL INGREDIENTS	COMBINE + SERVE
best basic homemade lemonade	*Start with 3 c. freshly squeezed lemon juice (about 12 juicy lemons).*	*Set aside:* ▸ *1 ¾ c. sugar*	*In a gallon-sized jug or pitcher, combine the lemon juice and sugar. Stir until the sugar dissolves.* *Add 12 c. water. Stir well. You can add ice to the jug, or serve over ice.*
ice-cold blueberry lemonade	*Start with 3 c. freshly squeezed lemon juice (about 12 juicy lemons).*	*Set aside:* ▸ *1 ¾ c. sugar* ▸ *3 c. fresh blueberries, washed well*	*In a gallon-sized jug or pitcher, combine the lemon juice and sugar. Stir until the sugar dissolves. Add the blueberries. Some people like to mash the berries a bit. I don't like the way it makes the lemonade cloudy with a lot of extra sediment, so I skip the mashing.* *Add 12 c. water. Stir well. You can add ice to the jug, or serve over ice.*

ice-cold mint lemonade	*Start with 3 c. freshly squeezed lemon juice (about 12 juicy lemons).*	*Set aside:*
		▸ *1 ¾ c. sugar*
		▸ *7 or 8 sprigs fresh mint (choose sprigs with plenty of leaves and wash them well)*
			In a gallon-sized jug or pitcher, combine the lemon juice and sugar. Stir until the sugar dissolves.
			    Add the mint.
			    Add 12 c. water. Stir well. You can add ice to the jug, or serve over ice.

ice-cold strawberry lemonade	*Start with 3 c. freshly squeezed lemon juice (about 12 juicy lemons).*	*Set aside:*
		▸ *1 ¾ c. sugar*
		Wash and hull 3 baskets strawberries (about 1½ lb. total). In a blender or food processor, puree 2 baskets of the straw-berries. Push through a sieve into a bowl and set aside. Cut the remaining 1 basket of straw-berries in half.
			In a gallon-sized jug or pitcher, combine the lemon juice, sugar, and strawberry puree. Stir until the sugar dissolves.
			    Add 12 c. water and the halved strawberries. Stir well. You can add ice to the jug, or serve over ice.
			    You can also make a version of this with pureed and whole raspberries.

ice-cold tropical lemonade	*Start with 3 c. freshly squeezed lemon juice (about 12 juicy lemons).*	*Set aside:*
		▸ *1 ¾ c. sugar*
		▸ *1 medium pineapple, peeled, cored, and cubed (about 3 c.).*
			In a gallon-sized jug or pitcher, combine the lemon juice and sugar. Stir until the sugar dissolves.
			    Add the pineapple and mash it a bit.
			    Add 12 c. water. Stir well. You can add ice to the jug, or serve over ice.

sangrías

I get a sparkle of delight in my eye when I see a glass of ruby red wine sangría dotted with jewels of ripe, juicy fruit – or, even better, a pale spritzy white wine sangría drunk with peach slices. Nothing declares a party better than a giant pitcher of this decadent drink. Serve up cold sangría on a warm summer evening outdoors, with plenty of good flavorful food, a bit of twilight atmosphere, and a spicy soundtrack.

Consider yourself warned, though: Sangría has a tendency to go down smooth and sweet, and before you know it your friends will end up sloshed and on their way to a sugar hangover they won't forgive you for the next morning.

The trick with sangría is striking the right balance. You want enough alcohol to pack a little punch, enough sugar to sweeten everything up, and the important melding of flavors that comes with time and patience. The further in advance you make sangría, the better it is. I make sangría days before a party. By the time the party is swinging, all the flavors have mellowed and melded together beautifully.

tips

- *Make your sangría with good-quality, super-ripe, juicy fruit.*
- *Serve sangría icy cold. Some people (and restaurants in particular) serve their sangría the same temperature they serve their wines. I don't like drenched room-temperature fruit, so I'm generous with the ice cubes.*
- *Serve your sangría with a ladle so that you get a balance of both fruit and wine in each glass.*
- *Go ahead and make your sangría a few days ahead of time. This allows you to get a jump-start on party preparations, and you end up with better sangría in the end.*

RUBY RED SANGRIÁ

STEP	1	2	3
TYPE OF SANGRIA	**PREP INGREDIENTS**	**ASSEMBLE INGREDIENTS**	**ADD FINISHING TOUCHES**
ruby red sangría	Set aside: ‣ 2 *oranges*, washed and sliced ‣ 2 *lemons*, washed and sliced ‣ ⅔ c. *sugar* ‣ Juice of 2 *oranges* ‣ ½ c. *Triple Sec* ‣ 2 bottles *red wine* (I like to use $7 to $10 Merlots)	In a gallon-sized container or jug, mash the orange and lemon slices a bit, together with the sugar. Add the orange juice and Triple Sec. Stir in the wine. Let the sangría sit in the fridge for at least a couple hours, preferably overnight.	Just before serving, add just a few handfuls of *ice* to the pitcher. You don't want to dilute the sangría.
midnight sangría	Set aside: ‣ 1 small basket *blackberries* ‣ 1 small basket *cherries*, stemmed and pitted ‣ 2 c. dark purple seedless *grapes* ‣ ½ c. *sugar* ‣ 1 shot *espresso* (optional) ‣ 2 bottles *red wine* (I like to use $7 to $10 Merlots) ‣ ½ c. *blackberry brandy*	In a gallon-sized container or jug, combine all the ingredients. Shake or stir well and let the sangría sit in the fridge for at least a couple hours, preferably overnight.	Pour into glasses full of *ice* and add a touch of *unsweetened sparkling water*.
very berry sangría	Set aside: ‣ 3 c. *raspberries* (red and golden, if possible) ‣ 1 c. washed, hulled, and sliced *strawberries* ‣ ⅓ c. *sugar* ‣ ½ c. *blackberry brandy* ‣ 2 c. white *cranberry juice* ‣ 2 bottles *white Zinfandel*	In a gallon-sized container or jug, combine all the ingredients. Shake or stir well and let the sangría sit in the fridge for at least a couple hours, preferably overnight.	Just before serving, add just a few handfuls of *ice* to the pitcher. You don't want to dilute the sangría.
white sangría with drunken peaches	Set aside: ‣ 2 to 3 *peaches*, sliced ‣ 3 c. seedless green and/or red *grapes*, cut in half ‣ ½ c. *sugar* ‣ 2 bottles *Sauvignon Blanc* ‣ ½ c. *apricot brandy*	In a gallon-sized container or jug, combine all the ingredients. Shake or stir well and let the sangría sit in the fridge for at least a couple hours, preferably overnight.	Pour into glasses full of *ice* with a generous splash of *unsweetened sparkling water*. Because you mix this sangría with a bit of bubbly water and ice cubes in individual glasses, don't put ice in the pitcher. You run the risk of the ice melting and diluting your sangría.

margaritas

I was caught off guard when I met an old friend for drinks late one afternoon in the East Village of New York City and ended up having the definitively perfect margarita. Keep in mind I'm a West Coast girl and no rookie when it comes to a good, cold, tequila-based cocktail. I've had margaritas in California, Puerto Vallarta, Baja, Tijuana, New Mexico, and any number of other places known for serving up a deluxe margarita. This one in particular was different — tasty ingredients, clever flavors, an extra step or two, and serious attention to little details made this margarita exceptional. I've been trying to replicate it ever since, and in the process I've dabbled with all sorts of new margarita flavors.

I typically like my margaritas on the rocks, but you can also make blended margaritas with these recipes. Just fill a blender three quarters full of ice, add a cup or two of the margarita mixture, and give it a good whirl.

BLENDED VERSUS ON THE ROCKS There are two entrenched margarita camps. Slushy, blended margaritas seem to maintain a stronghold at sorority spring break functions and Jimmy Buffett bashes. The more refined, on the rocks cocktail variety lends an option for many who might argue that blended margaritas only go with Tommy Bahama button-up shirts, poolside. I usually choose based on what time of day it is — slushy for days on the beach with girlfriends, on the rocks for a summer-evening cocktail party.

tips

- *Use decent tequila.*
- *If you don't finish off a pitcher, resist the urge to leave it out on the counter. Move it to the refrigerator, where it won't melt as quickly and it'll be ready for anyone who is up for seconds.*

- *To salt a margarita glass, run a wedge of lime around the rim and then dip the rim into a shallow pile of salt. Tap to shake off excess salt. Sugaring a glass rim works the same way.*

STEP	1	2	3
TYPE OF MARGARITA	PREP INGREDIENTS	COMBINE INGREDIENTS	ADD FINISHING TOUCHES
basic tequila margarita	Set aside: ‣ 2 c. *tequila* ‣ ⅔ c. *Triple Sec* ‣ ½ c. freshly squeezed **lime juice** ‣ 2 c. **lemonade**	Combine all the ingredients in a medium-sized pitcher and give them a good stir.	Fill the pitcher with ice and serve family style, or serve individually on the rocks in **salt**ed glasses garnished with **lime** wedges.
blood orange margarita	Set aside: ‣ 2 c. *tequila* ‣ ⅔ c. *Triple Sec* ‣ 1 ½ c. freshly squeezed **blood orange juice** ‣ Juice of 2 **limes**	Combine all the ingredients in a medium-sized pitcher and give them a good stir.	Fill the pitcher with ice and serve family style, or serve individually on the rocks in **suga**red glasses. These margaritas will also work with regular oranges.
hibiscus flower margarita	Bring to a boil: ‣ 1 c. **sugar** ‣ 1 c. dried **hibiscus flowers** ‣ 4 c. **water** As soon as the mixture begins to boil, turn the heat down to low and simmer for 10 minutes. Strain through cheesecloth or a fine-mesh sieve. Set aside to cool.	In a medium-sized pitcher, combine the cooled hibiscus syrup and 1 c. **tequila**. Stir well.	Fill the pitcher with ice and serve family style, or serve individually on the rocks in **salt**ed glasses garnished with **lime** wedges. I also like to use pretty pink and magenta **edible flowers** to garnish these margaritas.
pome- granate margarita	Set aside: ‣ 2 c. **tequila** ‣ 2 c. **pomegranate juice** ‣ ½ c. freshly squeezed **lime juice** ‣ ½ c. superfine **sugar**	Combine all the ingredients in a medium-sized pitcher and give them a good stir.	Fill the pitcher with ice and serve family style, or serve individually on the rocks in **salt**ed glasses garnished with **lime** wedges.
watermelon margarita	Set aside: ‣ 2 c. **tequila** ‣ 2 c. fresh **watermelon juice** (I just squeeze wedges of watermelon over a bowl, and then strain) ‣ ¼ c. freshly squeezed **lime juice** ‣ ½ c. **sugar** ‣ 2 T. **Triple Sec**	Combine all the ingredients in a medium-sized pitcher and give them a good stir.	Fill the pitcher with ice and serve family style, or serve individually on the rocks in **suga**red glasses. This also makes a great blended margarita.

IDEAS

garnishes / tabletop / menus /
flavor combinations

garnishes

Candy-cane hot chocolate stirrer

Add a little peppermint to your cocoa by using a candy-cane segment, a little cane, or a straight peppermint stick to stir.

Chives

Chives sprout some of the prettiest tiny purple-blue flowers you've ever seen. Use the flowers to garnish anything from a big bowl of mashed potatoes to soup or salad. And a quick party trick is to roll a small log of goat cheese in a bed of chopped chives. I grow chives on my back patio and I love to sprinkle them on all sorts of food for their zing of fresh onion flavor.

Cookie cutters

Use cookie cutters to add fun figures and shapes to cookies, pies, tarts, snacks, and tea sandwiches.

Edible flowers

You can buy little plastic containers of them at some markets now (as long as they don't look withered and sad, which defeats the purpose altogether), or grow your own at home.

Ice cube trays

Ice cube trays aren't just for making ice. I keep my eyes peeled for the malleable plastic ones in shapes like stars and fruit. I've used them as chocolate molds, and if you're really ambitious you can use them to shape butter pats or to make tiny popsicles.

Shaped cake pans

When presented the right way, shaped cakes can be delightful. I particularly like tiny shaped pans to use for cakes that are roughly 5 or 6 inches in diameter.

tabletop

Bread bowls

Nothing beats an individual-sized edible bowl. Take a round loaf of bread, such as sourdough, and cut off and reserve the top third. Hollow out the inside of the loaf, leaving the sides and bottom intact. Place the hollowed-out bread round and its top on a baking sheet and bake at 350° F for 10 minutes until lightly browned. Let it cool and fill with the soup or chowder of your choice.

Butcher paper

Butcher paper can be purchased in large rolls from many craft and supply stores. Use it as material for a tablecloth or placemat. Provide friends and family with crayons or colored pencils and watch them decorate their own table-tops. It's particularly fun for kids (and the young at heart). You can frame favorite sketches or make them part of future scrapbooks.

Edible arrangements

Instead of vases full of flowers, you can substitute tiny pots of edible herbs. If you can find herb plants that are flower-ing, even better. This is fun at a garden party, where guests can snip chives, basil, mint, and thyme straight from the table to garnish their food.

Edible place cards

I hardly ever have a need to assign seating, but I love this idea so much I'm including it here. Forget traditional paper place cards and play with edible ideas. Neatly spell out your guests' names on individual plates with sauce or infused olive oil, using a squeeze bottle. For kids, spell out names using alphabet cereal or pasta.

Fresh flowers

Fresh flower arrangements are an easy way to brighten up a table. I prefer to keep things very simple, often using only one type of flower or limiting my arrangements to a nar-row range of colors: all orange, all pink, all yellow.

White holiday lights

This works two ways. If you have a glass table, string sim-ple white holiday lights below it any time of the year for a festive look (you can even throw a sheer tablecloth over the table for a diffused glow). For outdoor, nonglass tables during nighttime festivities, loosely toss lights down the length of the table and then arrange them as you see fit with flowers or centerpieces.

FRESH FLOWERS

menus

Rise and shine brunch
Berry Fruit Bowl
Banana-Macadamia Pancakes
Mushroom Medley Frittata
Citrus Biscuits
Sparkling Peach Spritzer

Spring picnic
Zucchini Pocket Tarts
Artichoke Dip with baguette
Raspberry Tart
Nice bottle of white wine

Tailgate BBQ
Red Pepper + Lemon Kabobs
Hummus with pita wedges
Best Basic Iced Tea
Beer on ice

Deluxe brown-bag lunch
Brie, Apple-Cranberry + Fake Bacon Panini
Little bag of dried cranberries or apricots
A couple of Espresso Tuiles
Thermos of Best Basic Homemade Lemonade

Sky-high snacks (for long flights)
Roasted Vegetable Panini
A nice wedge of cheese
A couple squares of your favorite chocolate
Freeze a plastic bottle full of your favorite fruit-filled
spritzer and bring it with you. It will thaw en route.

Farmers' market Sunday supper
Citrus Risotto
Roasted Vegetables
Bright Green Pea + Mint Soup
Basic Tiny Greens with Olive Oil + Salt

Hot summer night patio party
Citrus Fruit Bowl
Guacamole
Salsa Fresca with fresh Homemade Tortillas
Butter Lettuce Sunshine Salad
Assorted Quesadillas
Ruby Red Sangría

Star-gazing date
Tapenade with baguette
Spring Butterflies with Lemon Cream
Roasted Asparagus
Freshest Berry Sherbet

Valentine's Day sweetheart dinner
Brie + Wild Mushroom Fondue
Herb Salad with Edible Flowers
Midnight Chocolate Tart
Your favorite bottle of wine to share

Après-ski fireside buffet
Wild Rice Bowl with Dried Cranberries
Red-Leaf Salad with Pomegranate Vinaigrette
Wild Mushroom Soup
Favorite Fettuccini Alfredo
Classic Berry Cobbler
Midnight Sangría

Girls' night in
Thin-Crust Pizzas (set up a make-your-own pizza bar)
Baby Spinach Salad with Mediterranean Goodies
Plenty of wine

flavor combinations SOME FAVORITE FLAVOR PAIRINGS + COMBINATIONS

Almonds
Almonds + apples
Almonds + caramel
Almonds + cream
Almonds + honey
Almonds + orange

Apples
Apples + almonds
Apples + brown sugar
Apples + caramel
Apples + cheese
Apples + cream
Apples + fennel
Apples + ginger
Apples + oats
Apples + pine nuts
Apples + walnuts

Apricots
Apricots + brandy
Apricots + caramel
Apricots + cherries
Apricots + chocolate
Apricots + cream
Apricots + oats
Apricots + pistachios
Apricots + vanilla

Asparagus
Asparagus + chiles
Asparagus + citrus
Asparagus + Parmesan
    or pecorino
Asparagus + toasted
    pine nuts

Basil
Basil + cinnamon
Basil + citrus
Basil + garlic
Basil + pine nuts
Basil + tomatoes

Carrots
Carrots + brown sugar
Carrots + oranges
Carrots + raisins or currants
Carrots + spices

Champagne
Champagne + cherries
Champagne + melon
Champagne + raspberries
Champagne + strawberries

Chocolate (dark)
Chocolate + apricots
Chocolate + bananas
Chocolate + berries
Chocolate + caramel
Chocolate + cherries
Chocolate + chiles
Chocolate + coffee
Chocolate + cream
Chocolate + macadamia nuts
Chocolate + mint
Chocolate + oats
Chocolate + vanilla
Chocolate + walnuts

Corn
Corn + butter
Corn + chiles
Corn + cream
Corn + Parmesan
Corn + peas

Fennel
Fennel + apples
Fennel + cheese
Fennel + citrus
Fennel + walnuts
Fennel + winter squashes

Ginger
Ginger + apples
Ginger + chiles
Ginger + cream
Ginger + melon
Ginger + mint
Ginger + oats
Ginger + pineapple
Ginger + winter squashes

Mint
Mint + chiles
Mint + citrus
Mint + feta
Mint + ginger
Mint + honey
Mint + melons
Mint + strawberries
Mint + summer squash
Mint + tea

Mushrooms
Mushrooms + cream
Mushrooms + garlic
Mushrooms + goat cheese
Mushrooms + herbs
Mushrooms + wine

Parmesan
Parmesan + asparagus
Parmesan + balsamic vinegar
Parmesan + corn
Parmesan + honey
Parmesan + lemon
Parmesan + pears

Pine nuts
Pine nuts + apples
Pine nuts + basil
Pine nuts + citrus
Pine nuts + goat cheese
Pine nuts + olives
Pine nuts + ricotta

Pumpkin
Pumpkin + apples
Pumpkin + brown sugar
Pumpkin + cream
Pumpkin + maple
Pumpkin + nuts
Pumpkin + oats
Pumpkin + raisins
Pumpkin + spices

Strawberries
Strawberries + balsamic
    vinegar
Strawberries + black pepper
Strawberries + brown sugar
Strawberries + champagne
Strawberries + chocolate
Strawberries + citrus
Strawberries + cream
Strawberries + mascarpone
Strawberries + mint
Strawberries + spices
Strawberries + vanilla
Strawberries + yogurt

Tomatoes
Tomatoes + basil (+ many
    other herbs)
Tomatoes + cheese
Tomatoes + chipotle chiles
Tomatoes + garlic
Tomatoes + olive oil
Tomatoes + olives

Vanilla
Vanilla + apricots
Vanilla + caramel
Vanilla + cherries
Vanilla + citrus
Vanilla + lavender
Vanilla + rose
Vanilla + strawberries

resources

Cowgirl Creamery
Great cheese.
www.cowgirlcreamery.com
Tel (707) 789-2604

Dean & DeLuca
www.deananddeluca.com
Tel (877) 826-9246
Fax (800) 781-4050

Eduardo's Pasta
One of my favorite brands of dried pasta.
Made in San Francisco, I now see their products
in quite a few markets.
Tel (415) 981-5082

JB Prince
An outrageous supply of molds, pots, pans, and machines.
www.jbprince.com
Tel (800) 473-0577

Mozzarella Company
www.mozzco.com
Tel (800) 798-2954

New England Cheesemaking Supply Company
www.cheesemaking.com
Tel (413) 628-3808

Penzeys Spices
Spice selections from around the world.
www.penzeys.com
Tel (800) 741-7787

The Perfect Puree
This Napa-based company supplies a long and delicious
list of high-quality flavors. Field-ripened berries, fruits, and
vegetables are pureed, frozen, and go on to make great
bases for everything from soups to sorbets.
www.perfectpuree.com
Tel (707) 261-5100

Ronald Reginald's
Premium vanilla beans, marinades, and extracts.
www.ronaldreginalds.com
Tel (800) 366-9766

Sugarcraft
Baking, candy, and decorating supplies.
www.sugarcraft.com

Sur La Table
All things kitchen and cooking related.
www.surlatable.com

Tierra Vegetables
Their jams are my favorites. Plenty of pesticide-free chiles
and preserves to choose from.
www.tierravegetables.com
Tel (888) 7-TIERRA

Trader Joe's
Look for a Trader Joe's in your area. My favorite things to pick
up there are olive oils, giant bars of chocolate, balsamic vinegar,
cheese, wine, dry pasta, and jars of roasted red peppers.
www.traderjoes.com

Vegan Supreme Marshmallows
www.vegansuprememarshmallows.com

Volcano Island Honey Company
My very favorite special-occasion honey. I like to treat myself
to a jar of their Rare Hawaiian Organic White Honey every
now and then.
www.volcanoislandhoney.com

conversion charts

weight equivalents

The metric weights given in this chart are not exact equivalents, but have been rounded up or down slightly to make measuring easier.

Avoirdupois	Metric
¼ oz	7 g
½ oz	15 g
1 oz	30 g
2 oz	60 g
3 oz	90 g
4 oz	115 g
5 oz	150 g
6 oz	175 g
7 oz	200 g
8 oz (½ lb)	225 g
9 oz	250 g
10 oz	300 g
11 oz	325 g
12 oz	350 g
13 oz	375 g
14 oz	400 g
15 oz	425 g
16 oz (1 lb)	450 g
1 ½ lb	750 g
2 lb	900 g
2 ¼ lb	1 kg
3 lb	1.4 kg
4 lb	1.8 kg

volume equivalents

These are not exact equivalents for American cups and spoons, but have been rounded up or down slightly to make measuring easier.

American	Metric	Imperial
¼ t	1.2 ml	
½ t	2.5 ml	
1 t	5.0 ml	
½ T (1.5 t)	7.5 ml	
1 T (3 t)	15 ml	
¼ cup (4 T)	60 ml	2 fl oz
⅓ cup (5 T)	75 ml	2 ½ fl oz
½ cup (8 T)	125 ml	4 fl oz
⅔ cup (10 T)	150 ml	5 fl oz
¾ cup (12 T)	175 ml	6 fl oz
1 cup (16 T)	250 ml	8 fl oz
1 ¼ cups	300 ml	10 fl oz (½ pt)
1 ½ cups	350 ml	12 fl oz
2 cups (1 pint)	500 ml	16 fl oz
2 ½ cups	625 ml	20 fl oz (1 pint)
1 quart	1 liter	32 fl oz

oven temperature equivalents

Oven Mark	F	C	Gas
Very cool	250-275	130-140	½ - 1
Cool	300	150	2
Warm	325	170	3
Moderate	350	180	4
Moderately hot	375	190	5
	400	200	6
Hot	425	220	7
	450	230	8
Very hot	475	250	9

index

Page numbers in **bold** refer to photographs

Apple:
-a-day smoothie, 22
brie pancakes, 32
cranberry, brie, and fake
bacon panini, **40**, 42
cranberry cobbler, 158
iced tea, spiced, 168
tart, **10**, 141
apricot(s):
summer fruit bowl, 24
summer tart with
macadamia shortbread
crust, 141
artichoke:
dip, 116
marinated, panini, 42
arugula, fig, and goat cheese
pizza, 59
asparagus:
Heidi's favorite stir-fry, 78
pizza verde, 60
roasted, 108
soup with Parmesan,
94, 96
spring butterflies with
lemon cream, 83
spring vegetable pot pie,
67
avocado, 23
butter lettuce sunshine
salad, **10**, 92
guacamole, 118
salsa, 128, **129**

Bacon, fake, brie apple
cranberry panini, **40**, 42
baking sheets, 15
balsamic:
berries, vanilla gelato
with, 149
vinaigrette, basic, 131
banana, 23
apple-a-day smoothie, 22
daiquiri sherbet, 145
honey bee smoothie, 22
macadamia pancakes,
31, 32
and PBJ panini, 43
sunrise smoothie, 22
triple-berry smoothie,
21, 22
tropical smoothie, 22

basil:
butter, 121
and goat cheese
mashed potatoes, 104
and lemon rice bowl
with tofu, 70
and Parmesan biscuits,
29
and tomato soup,
creamy, 97
see also pesto sauce
bean(s):
black, chowder, 100
fondue, spicy, 75
smashed black,
quesadillas, 46
spicy chili pot pie, 5,
65, 67
white, dip, 118
bean(s), long or green:
citrus tofu, and walnut
stir-fry, **77**, 78
and mushroom stir-fry,
spicy, 79
pretty summer salad, 93
berry(ies):
balsamic, vanilla gelato
with, 149
classic strawberry
shortcake, **137**, 138
cobbler, classic, **157**, 158
freshest, sherbet, **144**, 145
fruit bowl, 24, **25**
ice-cold strawberry
lemonade, 171
mascarpone pancakes, 33
midnight sangría, 174
mixed, shortcake, 138
raspberry tart, **6**, **140**, 143
sangría, very, 174
spritzer, sparkling mixed,
164
triple-berry smoothie,
21, 22
beverages, *see* drinks
biscuits, drop, 26, 27, 28-29
shortcakes, 136, **137**, 138
blackberry(ies):
berry fruit bowl, 24, 25
butter, 121
classic berry cobbler,
157, 158

freshest berry sherbet,
144, 145
midnight sangría, 174
mixed berry shortcake,
138
peach cobbler, 159
sparkling mixed berry
spritzer, 164
triple-berry smoothie,
21, 22
blender, 15
blueberry(ies):
berry fruit bowl, 24, 25
classic berry cobbler,
157, 158
lemonade, ice-cold, 171
sparkling mixed berry
spritzer, 164
bread:
bowls, 182
drop biscuits, **26**, 27,
28-29
homemade croutons, 16
breakfast, 18-37
drop biscuits, 26, 27,
28-29
frittatas, **34**, 35, 36-37
fruit bowls, 23, 24, **25**
pancakes, 30, **31**, 32-33
smoothies, 20, **21**, 22
butcher paper, 182
unsalted butter, 14
flavored, 119, **120**, 121-23

Cake pans, 15, 181
candy-cane hot chocolate
stirrer, **180**, 181
cantaloupe:
melon bowl, 24
melon sherbet, 146
sunrise smoothie, 22
carrots, roasted, **107**, 108
cheese, 14
apple-brie pancakes, 32
asparagus soup with
Parmesan, **94**, 96
berry-mascarpone
pancakes, 33
black olive quesadillas, 46
blue, butter, 121
blue, mixed greens with
walnuts and, 93

brie, apple-cranberry and
fake bacon panini,
40, 42
brie and wild mushroom
fondue, 74
chipotle fondue, 74
citrus-Parmesan
vinaigrette, 131
favorite fettuccini alfredo,
82
fondue, classic, 74
goat, and basil mashed
potatoes, 104
goat, and chive biscuits,
28
goat, and walnut panini,
42
goat, fondue, 75
goat, lemon vinaigrette,
132
goat, summer pot pie
with tomato and, 67
mashed sweet potatoes
with feta and chives,
105
panini margherita, 43
Parmesan and basil
biscuits, 29
quesadillas, basic, 46
red pepper and
gorgonzola butter, 123
saffron corkscrews with
peas and Parmesan, 83
smashed black bean
quesadillas, 46
thin-crust pizzas, 56-57,
58, 59-61
cherry(ies):
cobbler, 158
midnight sangría, 174
spritzer, sparkling, 164
summer fruit bowl, 24
tart with hazelnut
shortbread crust, 142
chickpea (garbanzo beans):
hummus, 116
and tomato chowder, 101
chile:
red, rice bowl with lime, 70
see also chipotle
chili:
pot pie, spicy, **5**, **65**, 66
spicy bean fondue, 75

chipotle:
  fire dip, 116
  fondue, 74
  mashed potatoes, 104
  potato pot pie, 66
chive(s), 181
  and goat cheese biscuits, 28
  lemon, and garlic butter, 122
  and lemon mashed potatoes, 104
  mashed sweet potatoes with feta and, 105
chocolate:
  fondue, 75
  sauce, mint-infused, vanilla gelato with, 150
  tart, midnight, 142
chowders, chunky, 98, **99**, 100-101
cilantro:
  lime vinaigrette, 132
  mashed sweet potatoes with lime and, 105
cinnamon:
  candies, crushed, vanilla gelato with, 149
  and spice biscuits, 28
  sugar quesadillas, **45**, 46
cobblers, 156, **157**, 158-59
coconut:
  corn, and curry soup, 96
  flakes, toasted, 16
  milk, 14
  milk, curried tofu in, 100
  tropical shortcake, 138
  tuiles, 154
  vanilla gelato with tropical toppings, **148**, 150
colander, 15
conversion charts, 187
cookie cutters, 15, 181
corn:
  chowder, spicy, 101
  coconut, and curry soup, 96
  kabobs, smoky, 55
  roasted, 108
cornmeal biscuits, 29
cranberry(ies):
  apple, brie, and fake bacon panini, **40**, 42

apple cobbler, 158
dried, wild rice bowl with, 2, **69**, 71
mustard vinaigrette, 131
  cream, sweetened fresh whipped, 16
croutons, homemade, 16
curry(ied):
  corn, and coconut soup, 96
  green, rice bowl with tofu, 70
  mango butter, 122
  tofu in coconut milk, 100
cutting board, 15

Daiquiri sherbet, 145
desserts, see sweets
dinners, one-dish, 62-87
  fondues, **72**, 73, 74-75
  pasta dishes, **80**, 81, 82-83
  pot pies, **5**, 64, **65**, 66-67
  rice bowls, 2, 68, **69**, 70-71
  risottos, 84, **85**, 86-87
  stir-fries, 76, **77**, 78-79
dips, 114, **115**, 116-18
  salsas, 127, 128, **129**
drinks, 160-77
  iced teas, 165, **166**, 167-68
  lemonades, 169, **170**, 171
  margaritas, 175, **176**, 177
  sangrías, 172, **173**, 174
  smoothies, 20, **21**, 22
  spritzers, **162**, 163, 164

Edible arrangements, 182
edible flowers, 181
edible place cards, 182
eggplant, roasted, 109
eggs, 14
  frittatas, **34**, 35, 36-37
electric mixer and food processor, 15
equipment, 15
espresso:
  tuiles, 154
  vanilla gelato with, 149

Fig, arugula and goat cheese pizza, 59
flavor combinations, 185
flower arrangements, **4**, 182, **183**

flowers, edible, 181
fondues, **72**, 73, 74-75
food processor, 15
frittatas, **34**, 35, 36-37
fruit(s):
  bowls, 23, 24, **25**
  cobblers, 156, **157**, 158-59
  dried, 14
  selecting, 23
  tarts, 6, **10**, 139, **140**, 141-43
  see also specific fruits

Garlic, 14
  lemon, and chive butter, 122
  roasted, 16
  ultra roasted, mashed potatoes, 105
  roasted, vinaigrette, 133
garbanzo bean (chickpeas):
  hummus, 116
  and tomato chowder, 101
garnishes, **180**, 181
gelato, vanilla, with toppings, 147, **148**, 149-50
ginger:
  gingersnap tuiles, 155
  iced tea, 167
grapefruit:
  champagne vinaigrette, 132
  citrus fruit bowl, 24
grater, 15
greens:
  Asian, noodles stir-fried with, 79
  mixed, stir-fry, 79
  salads, 8, **10**, 90, **91**, 92-93
guacamole, 118

Hazelnut(s):
  shortbread crust, cherry tart with, 142
  toasted, 16
herb pots, 182
hibiscus flower margarita, **176**, 177
holiday lights, 182
honey:
  bee smoothie, 22
  biscuits, 29
  lime butter, 122
hummus, 116

Ice cube trays, 181
iced teas, 165, **166**, 167-68
ideas, 178-85
  flavor combinations, 185
  garnishes, **180**, 181
  menus, 184
  tabletop, **4**, 182, **183**
ingredients, 14

Kabobs, savory, 51, 52, **53**, 54-55
knives, 15

Leek-potato pocket tarts, 48
lemon:
  and basil rice bowl with tofu, 70
  and chive mashed potatoes, 104
  citrus biscuits, 28
  citrus risotto, **85**, 86
  citrus sunshine iced tea, 167
  cream, spring butterflies with, 83
  garlic, and chive butter, 122
  goat cheese vinaigrette, 132
  lemonades, 169, **170**, 171
  poppy seed pancakes, 33
  and red pepper kabobs, **53**, 54
  ruby red sangría, **173**, 174
  sparkling citrus spritzer, **162**, 164
lemonades, 169, **170**, 171
lentil, red, dip, **115**, 117
lights, holiday, 182
lime:
  cilantro vinaigrette, 132
  honey butter, 122
  mashed sweet potatoes with cilantro and, 105
  raspberry spritzer, sparkling, 164
  red chile rice bowl with, 70
  watermelon smoothie, 22
lunch, 38-61
  panini, **40**, 41, 42-43
  pocket tarts, **47**, 48-50
  quesadillas, 44, **45**, 46

savory kabobs, 51, 52, 53, 54-55

thin-crust pizzas, 56-57, **58**, 59-61

Macadamia nut(s):

banana pancakes, **31**, 32

shortbread crust, apricot summer tart with, 141

vanilla gelato with tropical toppings, **148**, 150

mango, 23

curry butter, 122

rice bowl, spiced, 71

tropical shortcake, 138

margaritas, 175, **176**, 177

marshmallow fondue, 75

measuring spoons and cups, 15

melon(s), 23

bowl, 24

sherbet, 146

sunrise smoothie, 22

watermelon-lime smoothie, 22

watermelon margarita, 177

menus, 184

mint:

and feta pizza, 59

iced tea, 168

-infused chocolate sauce, vanilla gelato with, 150

lemonade, ice-cold, 171

orange vinaigrette, 133

and pea soup, bright green, 96

pumpkin, and ricotta pizza, 61

mixer, electric, 15

muffin tins, 15

mushroom(s):

and green bean stir-fry, spicy, 79

kabobs, 54

medley frittata, **34**, 36

pot pie, creamy, 66

roasted portobello, 110

sautéed, sauce, 126

wild, and brie fondue, 74

wild, pocket tarts, 50

wild, soup, 97

mustard:

basic French vinaigrette, **130**, 131

cranberry vinaigrette, 131

olive butter, 122

Noodles:

stir-fried with Asian greens, 79

see also pasta

nuts, 14

apricot summer tart with macadamia shortbread crust, 141

banana-macadamia pancakes, **31**, 32

cherry tart with hazelnut shortbread crust, 142

citrus tofu, long bean and walnut stir-fry, **77**, 78

goat cheese and walnut panini, 42

mixed greens with blue cheese and walnuts, 93

pistachio butter, **120**, 123

pumpkin-walnut pancakes, 33

toasted, 16

toasted, and olive pizza, 61

toasted pine nut and kalamata olive butter, 123

vanilla gelato with tropical toppings, **148**, 150

Olive(s), 14

black, quesadillas, 46

kalamata, and toasted pine nut butter, 123

mustard butter, 122

and red pepper pizza, 61

tapenade, 117

and toasted nuts pizza, 61

olive oil, 14

onions, 14

roasted, 109

orange(s):

blood, margarita, 177

blood, sherbet, 145

blood, vinaigrette, 131

butter lettuce sunshine salad, **10**, 92

citrus biscuits, 28

citrus fruit bowl, 24

citrus-Parmesan vinaigrette, 131

citrus risotto, **85**, 86

citrus sunshine iced tea, 167

citrus tofu, long bean and walnut stir-fry, **77**, 78

citrus tuiles, 152

mint vinaigrette, 133

ruby red sangría, **173**, 174

sparkling citrus spritzer, **162**, 164

sunrise smoothie, 22

Pancakes, 30, **31**, 32-33

panini, **40**, 41, 42-43

pans, 15

parchment paper, 15

pasta, 14, 81

dishes, **80**, 81, 82-83

pastes and sauces, prepared, 14

pea(s):

and mint soup, bright green, 96

saffron corkscrews with Parmesan and, 83

peach(es), 23

blackberry cobbler, 159

drunken, white sangría with, 174

honey bee smoothie, 22

sherbet, 146

spritzer, sparkling, 164

summer fruit bowl, 24

peanut dip, spicy, 118

peanut oil, 14

pepper(s), red:

and gorgonzola butter, 123

and lemon kabobs, **53**, 54

and olive pizza, 61

puree soup, 97

roasted, 110

roasted, dip, 117

sauce, 126

vinaigrette, 133

peppermint stick chocolate stirrer, **180**, 181

pesto sauce, 126

and new potato pizza, 60

pizza verde, 60

pies, pot, **5**, 64, **65**, 66-67

pineapple:

butter, 123

daiquiri sherbet, 145

ice-cold tropical lemonade, 171

rum cobbler, 159

salsa, tropical, 128

spicy Hawaiian kabobs, 55

tropical shortcake, 138

tropical smoothie, 22

vanilla gelato with tropical toppings, **148**, 150

pine nut(s):

toasted, and kalamata olive butter, 123

toasted, and olive pizza, 61

pistachio butter, **120**, 123

pizzas, thin-crust, 56-57, **58**, 59-61

place cards, edible, 182

plum tart, rustic, 143

pomegranate:

iced tea, 168

margarita, 177

vinaigrette, 133

vinaigrette, red-leaf salad with, 8, **91**, 93

poppy seed-lemon pancakes, 33

potato(es):

chipotle pot pie, 66

chowder, rustic, **99**, 100

leek pocket tarts, 48

mashed, **102**, 103, 104-5

new, and pesto pizza, 60

roasted new, 109

tri-color, frittata, 37

pot pies, 5, 64, **65**, 66-67

pots, 15

pumpkin:

mint, and ricotta pizza, 61

walnut pancakes, 33

Quesadillas, 44, **45**, 46

Raspberry(ies):

berry fruit bowl, 24, 25

classic berry cobbler, **157**, 158

cobbler, simple, 159

freshest berry sherbet, **144**, 145

lime spritzer, sparkling, 164

mixed berry shortcake, 138

sparkling mixed berry spritzer, 164

tart, 6, **140**, 143

triple-berry smoothie, **21**, 22

very berry sangría, 174

resources, 186

rice, 14

bowls, 2, 68, **69**, 70-71

risottos, 84, **85**, 86-87

risottos, 84, **85**, 86-87

Saffron:

corkscrews with peas and Parmesan, 83

mashed potatoes, **102**, 105

salads, green, **8**, **10**, 90, 91, 92-93

salsas, 127, 128, **129**

salt, 14

sandwiches:

panini, **40**, 41, 42-43

quesadillas, 44, **45**, 46

sangrías, 172, **173**, 174

sauces, 124, **125**, 126

salsas, 127, 128, **129**

vinaigrettes, **130**, 130, 131-33

sauces and pastes, prepared, 14

sesame, toasted, rice bowl, 71

shallots, 14

sherbets, **144**, 145-46

shortcakes, 136, **137**, 138

sides, 88-111

chunky chowders, 98, **99**, 100-101

green salads, **8**, **10**, 90, **91**, 92-93

mashed potatoes, **102**, 103, 104-5

roasted vegetables, 106, **107**, 108-11

smooth soups, **94**, 95, 96-97

silicone baking mat, 15

smoothies, 20, **21**, 22

soups:

chunky chowders, 98, **99**, 100-101

smooth, **94**, 95, 96-97

spices, 14

spinach:

baby, salad with Mediterranean goodies, 92

frittata, 37

pocket tarts, 49

wilted, whole wheat penne with, 83

spoon, wooden, 15

spreads:

dips, 114, **115**, 116-18

flavored butters, 119, **120**, 121-23

salsas, 127, 128, **129**

spritzers, **162**, 163, 164

squash:

butternut, kabobs, 52

fall vegetable pot pie, 66

pumpkin, mint and ricotta pizza, 61

pumpkin-walnut pancakes, 33

roasted winter, 111

roasted zucchini, 111

zucchini pocket tarts, 50

staple items, 14

stir-fries, 76, **77**, 78-79

stockpile, 14

strawberry(ies):

balsamic, vanilla gelato with, 149

freshest berry sherbet, **144**, 145

lemonade, ice-cold, 171

mixed berry shortcake, 138

shortcake, classic, **137**, 138

sparkling mixed berry spritzer, 164

triple-berry smoothie, **21**, 22

very berry sangría, 174

vodka sherbet, 146

watermelon-lime smoothie, 22

sugar:

brown, butter, 121

cinnamon quesadillas, **45**, 46

sweet potatoes:

mashed, with feta and chives, 105

mashed, with lime and cilantro, 105

roasted, 110

sweets, 134-59

cobblers, 156, **157**, 158-59

sherbets, 144, **144**, 145-46

shortcakes, 136, **137**, 138

tarts, 6, **10**, 139, **140**, 141-43

tuiles, 151, 152, **153**, 154-55

vanilla gelato with toppings, 147, **148**, 149-50

Tabletop ideas, **4**, 182, 183

tapenade, 117

tart pans, 15

tarts:

fruit, **6**, **10**, 139, **140**, 141-43

pocket, **47**, 48-50

teas, iced, 165, **166**, 167-68

thermometer, oven, 15

tofu:

citrus, long bean and walnut stir-fry, **77**, 78

curried, in coconut milk, 100

green curry rice bowl with, 70

Heidi's favorite stir-fry, 78

lemon and basil rice bowl with, 70

tomatillo(s):

avocado salsa, 128, **129**

roasted, 111

salsa, 128

tomato(es), 14

and basil soup, creamy, 97

cherry, broken lasagna with, **80**, 82

and chickpea chowder, 101

heirloom, frittata, 36

panini margherita, 43

pocket tarts, 49

pretty summer salad, 93

risotto, 87

salsa fresca, 128

spicy chili pot pie, **5**, **65**, 67

summer pot pie with goat cheese and, 67

sun-dried, dip, 118

tomato sauce, bright red, **125**, 126

pasta with, 82

simple pizza margherita, **58**, 59

toasted nuts and olive pizza, 61

tuiles, 151, 152, **153**, 154-55

Vanilla:

gelato with toppings, 147, **148**, 149-50

tuiles, 155

vegetable(s):

roasted, 106, **107**, 108-11

roasted, panini, 43

see also specific vegetables

vinaigrettes, 130, **130**, 131-33

Walnut(s):

citrus tofu, and long bean stir-fry, **77**, 78

and goat cheese panini, 42

mixed greens with blue cheese and, 93

pumpkin pancakes, 33

watermelon, 23

lime smoothie, 22

margarita, 177

whipped cream, sweetened fresh, 16

Yams, roasted, 110

Zucchini:

pocket tarts, 50

roasted, 111